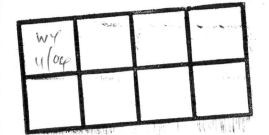
Gluten-*free* food

D0230906

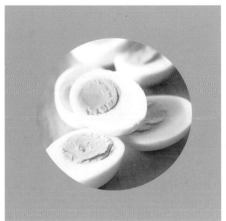

Lyndel Costain & Joanna Farrow

Coeliac UK Mission Statement:
To support the health, welfare and rights of Coeliacs, those with Dermititis Herpetiformis (D.H.) and other medically diagnosed patients whose health and quality of life can be improved by following the dietary regime beneficial to Coeliacs.
To provide easily accessible written, verbal and electronic advice, information and resources to these individuals or groups.
To educate the public and those in appropriate sectors of health, government, commerce and industry on the conditions and the issues.
To promote and commission research into the causes, alleviation, treatment, care and cure of the Coeliac and D.H. conditions.

Lyndel Costain B.Sc.SRD is an award-winning state registered dietitian health writer and broadcaster on television and radio. She is passionate about the importance of correctly diagnosing and treating the often overlooked condition of gluten intolerance (or coeliac disease). Lyndel has 17 years experience, is a past spokesperson for the British Dietetic Association, and regularly writes for professional and popular books and magazines.

Joanna Farrow trained as a home economist and worked for several years on women's magazines. She is now a freelance writer and works for a range of food magazines including *BBC Good Food*. Joanna has written a diverse range of cookery books and also styles food for photography.

First published in Great Britain in 2003 by Hamlyn,
a division of Octopus Publishing Group Ltd
2–4 Heron Quays, London E14 4JP

Copyright © Octopus Publishing Group Ltd 2003

ISBN 0 600 60793 3

A CIP catalogue record for this book is available from the British Library

Printed and bound in China

10 9 8 7 6 5 4 3 2 1

NOTES
This books includes dishes made with nuts and nut derivatives. It is advisable for those with known allergic reactions to nuts and nut derivatives and those who may be potentially vulnerable to these allergies, such as pregnant and nursing mothers, invalids, the elderly, babies and children, to avoid dishes made with nuts and nut oils. It is also prudent to check the labels of preprepared ingredients for the possible inclusion of nut derivatives.

All the recipes in this book have been analysed by a professional nutritionist. The calcium and iron content may vary if non-dairy alternatives are used in place of dairy milk, butter and cream.

Contents

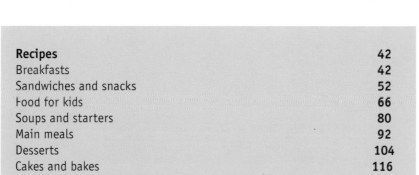

Introduction

Following a gluten-free diet means you will always have to choose and cook gluten-free food.

Symbols used in this book

 gluten-free

 wheat-free

 cows' milk-free

 egg-free

 nut-free

 suitable for vegetarians

This book offers practical help for anyone who suffers from gluten intolerance. It gives clear advice on how to ensure accurate diagnosis of symptoms, and explains how you can continue to enjoy a healthy and varied diet. Most importantly, it provides a comprehensive guide for people with coeliac disease, which is a lifelong, genetically linked condition that can affect people of any age, sex or ethnicity. If the problem is not treated with a strict gluten-free diet, it can have serious and wide-ranging health implications. It is also much more common than was once thought and is greatly under-diagnosed.

Anyone who has had to change their diet for health reasons will know what an impact this has on day-to-day life. You will need to check and be sure of everything you eat and friends and family will also need to understand the importance and practicalities of the changes involved.

Before you even reach this stage, actually identifying gluten intolerance can be hard work. Food intolerance is a difficult area, partly because of a limited understanding of the subject and partly because of the lack of reliable food intolerance tests. People may spend a lot of time and money looking for an answer to their health problems, without finding effective help and possibly compromising their nutritional intake in the process.

However, the good news is that there are clear diagnostic tests for coeliac disease. There are also sensible, safe ways to investigate wheat allergy and intolerance. This book will give you the confidence to assess and deal with your symptoms. It also provides an extensive range of mouthwatering recipes to ensure that your tastebuds never have to suffer. This means you will be in a position to take charge of your own health and well-being – for life.

THE RECIPES

All of the recipes in this book can be used by anyone on a gluten-free or a wheat-free diet and are suitable for everyone, apart from babies. Make a note of your favourites, as this will be useful for friends or relatives who want to cook for you. The symbols shown on the left appear at the top of each recipe, so you can see at a glance what is suitable if you have other dietary needs. It is important to check that ready-made ingredients such as mustard, ketchup, soy sauce, fish sauce and chocolate, are gluten-free.

Keeping a good nutritional balance can be difficult if your diet is restricted in some way. This book offers advice on how to make sure you get all the key vitamins and minerals you need and how to protect against long-term health problems such as obesity, heart disease and osteoporosis.

Recipes can be adapted to suit different dietary requirements. To reduce the
fat content, use skimmed or semi-skimmed milk, low-fat yogurts, half-fat
cream cheeses, sour cream and crème fraîche, reduced fat coconut milk,
whipping cream in place of double cream and low calorie mayonnaise. You
could also reduce the amount of oil used. To limit your saturated fat intake,
switch butter for spreads labelled low in saturates, such as olive oil-based
spreads. If you are following a lactose-free diet, substitute butter for dairy-
free margarine; and yogurt, milk and cream for dairy-free versions such as
soya (or rice) milks, creams and yogurts.

The five main food groups required for a balanced diet

Fruit and vegetables

Bread, cereals and potatoes

**Meat, fish
and other protein foods**

Milk and dairy foods

Fats, oils and sugary foods

This chart shows the five food groups that contribute to a balanced and
varied diet in the healthiest proportions. By choosing suitable foods from
each group every day, you will get the nutrients you need.

Adverse reactions to food

FOOD ALLERGY

Some people produce excessive amounts of an antibody called immunoglobulin E (IgE) when they eat or inhale allergens, which could be certain foods (milk, nuts, fish and eggs are common offenders), pollens, dust or animal fur. They are described as being 'atopic', a condition that tends to run in families. This rapidly causes allergic reactions such as a runny nose, wheezing, urticaria (hives or nettle rash), flushing, swelling of the face or, in extreme cases, life-threatening anaphylaxis. Atopic people can also have more delayed reactions to foods, when symptoms such as eczema, asthma, diarrhoea or migraine do not appear for several hours or days.

It is also possible to have food allergies that are not triggered by IgE antibodies but by other parts of the immune system. Again the symptoms can be delayed. The best-known example of this type of food allergy is coeliac disease, a condition in which the bowel reacts adversely to gluten.

FOOD INTOLERANCE

Food intolerance differs from food allergy in that the allergic reactions it causes do not involve the immune system. There are a number of different types:

● **Enzyme problems** The most common example of this is when people lack lactase, the enzyme needed to digest lactose, the sugar found in milk. Sometimes people with coeliac disease have lactose intolerance (see page 36).

● **Food aversion** This is where people avoid a food either for psychological reasons or because they link it to feeling ill. For example, if someone was coincidentally very sick after eating a certain food, they may be put off eating that food again.

● **Ingredient or chemical sensitivity** Certain substances in food can provoke symptoms in susceptible people. For example, tyramine in matured cheese and red wine may cause migraine or flushing, and the preservative sulphur dioxide may aggravate asthma.

● **Other causes** This is where wheat intolerance is most likely to fit. There is much debate at present about whether proteins in the offending food make the lining of the bowel 'leaky', allowing them to enter the bloodstream and cause symptoms. Upsetting the natural balance of bacteria in the bowel may also have a key role to play in these less well-understood types of food intolerance.

Some people have unpleasant allergic reactions when they eat certain foods.

Gluten and coeliac disease

WHAT IS GLUTEN?

Coeliac disease is caused by the body reacting badly to gluten, a type of protein found predominantly in wheat. Gluten becomes sticky and malleable when combined with water, meaning that it is ideal for bread-making. Gluten itself comprises many different proteins, the best-known of which is gliadin. This is the part of gluten that triggers the immune reaction. Proteins in rye, barley and possibly oats (see page 18) are very similar to gliadin and they too damage the bowel of people with coeliac disease.

In the case of wheat allergy, the body also reacts badly to different proteins found in wheat. However, these have not been as well researched and identified as the proteins that trigger coeliac disease and the related condition dermatitis herpetiformis (see page 8).

WHEN DID GLUTEN INTOLERANCE START?

Human beings have been on earth for many thousands of years, but for most of this time they were hunters and gatherers, trapping animals, catching fish and collecting wild vegetables, fruit, seeds and herbs. Only quite recently in evolutionary terms – about 10,000 years ago – did groups of our ancestors learn how to domesticate plants and animals, and as a result form stable settlements.

This was the beginning of agriculture, and would have seen the first appearance of crops of gluten-containing wheat and barley. It would also have seen the first appearance of what we know today as coeliac disease. For some reason, certain people were not able to tolerate this new protein in their diet.

As agriculture became established around the world, only populations that grew wheat and barley were affected in this way. Large areas of the world where rice, maize, millet and sorghum were the main grains would have been, and still are, essentially, unaffected. But as our populations move and intermingle, so the genetic potential for coeliac disease increases.

Gluten is a type of protein found predominantly in wheat.

Coeliac disease explained

The word 'coeliac' is derived from the Greek koiliakos, which means 'of the bowels'.

Coeliac disease is a genetically linked condition caused by a lifelong intolerance to gluten in wheat and similar proteins in rye, barley and possibly oats. When people with coeliac disease eat gluten-containing foods, their immune system fights the gluten, causing inflammation of the delicate cells lining the small intestine. In the process, the small intestine's villi – finger-like projections necessary for the absorption of nutrients and fluid from food and drink – become flattened and cannot do their job properly, causing digestive and nutritional upsets.

WHO GETS COELIAC DISEASE?

A report in the journal *Gastroenterology* estimated that as many as one in 260 people worldwide may have coeliac disease. It is most common in areas where a lot of wheat is eaten. In America and some European countries, for example, it affects between 0.5 and 1 per cent of the population. However, since coeliac disease is under-diagnosed, a lot of people will not be aware they have it. According to Coeliac UK, although only about 50,000 sufferers in Britain have been diagnosed, another 500,000 have the condition.

Coeliac disease runs in families and can begin at any age, even though the person has previously eaten gluten without any problem. In addition to a genetic predisposition and eating gluten, some sort of trigger, such as a bad accident, a viral infection or even pregnancy, may set it off.

DERMATITIS HERPETIFORMIS

Dermatitis herpetiformis (DH) results in itchy blisters mainly on the back of the elbows and forearms, the buttocks and the front of the knees. In the 1960s it was shown that people with DH also have a very mild form of coeliac disease. Until then, DH had been treated with medication, but now a gluten-free diet is prescribed instead. This may take up to 6 months to have an effect, however, so medication may be used as well for the first few months.

DH is first investigated by examining the skin for a substance called immunoglobulin A (IgA). Diagnosis is then confirmed using the tests for coeliac disease (see page 12). It too is a lifelong condition and has a genetic basis, but is much rarer than coeliac disease, affecting about one in 15,000 people. It is possible for coeliac disease sufferers to develop DH, but the risk is greatly decreased if they follow a gluten-free diet.

People with coeliac disease must avoid (clockwise from top left) barley, wheat, rye and possibly oats.

Coeliac disease is most common in countries where a lot of wheat-based foods are eaten.

Symptoms

The symptoms of coeliac disease can vary greatly, which is why so many people remain undiagnosed. The most common are diarrhoea, tiredness, anaemia, bloating, wind, low mood and weight loss, all of which may come and go. When people think back, they often realize that they have had some symptoms since childhood.

Some babies who have been healthy from birth may become irritable, anaemic and fail to grow properly once gluten-containing cereals are introduced. Others may not have problems until they are toddlers. Diarrhoea, developing a potbelly and passing smelly, pale stools that are difficult to flush away (because they contain fat that the child has not absorbed) are other common signs of coeliac disease.

In the past, the condition was recognized only when people were ill. These days, because a lot more is known about it, 'silent' cases (when there are no obvious symptoms) are sometimes picked up during routine blood tests for, say, anaemia or irritable bowel syndrome. Once people with 'silent' coeliac disease start a gluten-free diet, they usually feel a lot more energetic.

Coeliac disease is also linked to other health problems. Studies show that half of all newly diagnosed patients did not come to see their doctor initially because of bowel symptoms. The list on the right shows the conditions that could develop if coeliac disease remains untreated (note, though, that there are also other reasons why these conditions might develop).

CAN COELIAC DISEASE BE PREVENTED?

When coeliac disease was first recognized, it was seen largely as a problem for young children, but since the mid-1970s fewer children and more adults have been diagnosed. This is thought to be because more women are breast-feeding their babies (thus helping to strengthen the bowel and immune system), and also because more babies are being weaned on to gluten-free foods. Babies' immune systems are still quite fragile in the first few months of life and gluten could trigger coeliac disease if they are genetically predisposed to it.

Recent research in Sweden found that the risk of coeliac disease was reduced by 40 per cent in children under two if the children were still breast-fed when first given gluten-containing foods. The reduction increased to 65 per cent if they continued to be breast-fed while having gluten-containing foods. However, studies of this sort do not tell us if coeliac disease was actually eliminated or simply postponed.

Related conditions

The following are conditions that may develop if coeliac disease is left untreated:

- Mouth ulcers
- Sore tongue
- Nausea, poor appetite
- Stomach pain
- Vitamin and mineral deficiencies
- Depression and anxiety
- Weak bones (osteoporosis)
- Cramps
- Rheumatoid arthritis
- Hair loss
- Weakened tooth enamel
- Susceptibility to infections
- Easy bruising
- Difficulty getting pregnant
- Repeated miscarriage
- Not reaching full height potential
- Skin problems such psoriasis and eczema
- Liver disease
- Tingling in the hands and feet
- Epilepsy
- Ataxia (a disorder of the nervous system)
- Psychiatric disturbances

Investigation and treatment

We have already seen that coeliac disease is under-diagnosed, but it is still the case that much more is known about it than about wheat intolerance. In fact, some nutritionists are not sure if wheat intolerance, as distinct from gluten intolerance, exists. Since the two share some common symptoms – tiredness, low mood and bowel upsets, for example – it is quite possible that what people think of as wheat intolerance is actually coeliac disease. This makes it absolutely vital to ensure that coeliac disease is properly diagnosed and then treated with a gluten-free, not just a wheat-free, diet to protect future health.

If you suspect that you or a member of your family reacts badly to wheat, then your first step should be to see your doctor. It really helps to take along a food and symptom diary (see below). Based on your general health, medical history and food diary, your doctor will be able to make decisions about whether wheat allergy or intolerance or coeliac disease is your problem. If wheat allergy – where the immune system is involved – is suspected, you can be referred for medical food allergy tests. If positive, the results will need confirming with a medically supervised wheat challenge. You will then need to follow a wheat-free diet (see page 16).

When it comes to wheat intolerance, there are at present no medical tests that give a reliable diagnosis. You will have to try removing wheat from your diet and noting how your symptoms change. Unorthodox approaches such as hair analysis, pulse tests, sweat tests and kinesiology have no proven scientific basis and are not recommended by health professionals.

Bread is one of the most common sources of wheat in the diet.

FOOD AND SYMPTOM DIARY

If you suspect that wheat upsets you in some way, keep a food and symptom diary (see opposite) for a few weeks to get a clearer picture. Fill the diary in throughout the day, as it is very hard to remember what you have eaten after the event. Record absolutely everything you eat and drink, including any medicines and supplements.

INVESTIGATING WHEAT INTOLERANCE

If you have reactions that take hours or days to develop, or are always present, and you feel that wheat may be responsible, you can investigate using this approach:

● Follow a wheat-free diet for three weeks. If you have any other medical problems, check with your doctor first. You may also benefit from the help of a qualified dietician. Plan ahead to ensure that you have the right foods in the

Date	Time	Food and Drink	Symptoms	Time	Severity Rating*
4th May	8 a.m.	2 slices of toast with jam	Stomach cramp	11 a.m.	2
		Orange juice	Feel tired	All morning	3
			*Symptoms should be given one of the following ratings:		
			1 = mild, 2 = moderate, 3 = bad, 4 = severe		

house and choose a time when it is easiest from a social point of view to follow the diet. Keep up your food and symptom diary.

● If there is no improvement in your symptoms, then wheat intolerance is unlikely to be the problem. However, coeliac disease (or another food allergy/intolerance) is still a possibility, so discuss this with your doctor.

● If your symptoms improve or disappear, then reintroduce wheat* to see if they come back – this is known as a wheat challenge (see below). If they do return, then wheat intolerance is possible. However, so is coeliac disease.

● Make an appointment to see your doctor to discuss whether or not you have coeliac disease. Take along your food and symptom diary. If wheat intolerance is diagnosed, then you will need to follow a wheat-free diet (see page 16). If coeliac disease is your problem, you will need a gluten-free diet.

Wheat challenge

● Retry wheat for at least three days – or for a week if eczema and migraine are your symptoms.

● Any foods that are 100 per cent wheat are suitable: for example, 100 per cent wheat pasta, cereal or crackers.

● Eat a little more of the food every day.

● If you have no reaction, then keep eating the food. If you have a reaction, stop eating it and arrange to see your doctor.

*Food challenges should never be attempted with children, or if there is any risk or history of anaphylaxis, without medical supervision.

100 per cent wheat foods, such as pasta, are the most suitable for a 'wheat challenge'.

INVESTIGATING COELIAC DISEASE

You should talk to your doctor about being tested for coeliac disease if:

- You seem to react badly to wheat.
- You have been suffering from any or a number of the symptoms described on page 9 and there is no other medically confirmed reason for them, or you are not feeling better after being treated for a medical reason.
- Someone in your family has coeliac disease, even if you do not have any symptoms.
- You have Type 1 diabetes (see page 35).

There are two types of test used to investigate and diagnose coeliac disease. First, there are blood tests that look for specific antibodies. You must ensure that you have eaten a normal gluten-containing diet for a couple of weeks leading up to the test. If the tests are positive, it is very likely, though not definite, that you have coeliac disease. Occasionally, antibody tests on people who have coeliac disease appear normal (a false negative test) while those on people who do not have it show raised antibody levels (a false positive test). To help make sense of the antibody tests, your doctor will also look for other common problems, such as anaemia. If all of the above tests are negative but your symptoms persist, it is wise to be retested in the future. This is especially important for children.

A second test is required for a final and definite diagnosis. A gastroenterologist will carry out a quick and painless biopsy of the small intestine. If damage is found, coeliac disease is confirmed.

TREATMENT

This book should be used in addition to the advice you get from your dietician and doctor rather than being seen as an alternative. Lifestyles differ and people have different dietary and medical requirements. Your dietician will be able to provide advice that is tailored to your particular situation and will know how to answer your specific questions. They will also have information about local support groups.

Seek advice from your doctor if you think you may be suffering from coeliac disease.

Once the diagnosis of coeliac disease or dermatitis herpetiformis (see page 8) is confirmed, your gastroenterologist will refer you to a dietician who will explain the principles and importance of a gluten-free diet and give practical guidance on following it on a day-to-day basis. If you have coeliac disease you will need to follow your diet for life, even when you feel well. This is because a lack of obvious symptoms does not mean that gluten is not affecting the bowel and so increasing the risk of health problems.

Most people with obvious symptoms find that they start to feel better within days of beginning their gluten-free diet. Lost weight is gradually regained – sometimes very quickly, as improved well-being means a bigger appetite – and energy levels increase, regardless of how healthy they felt beforehand.

If you continue to feel unwell after a few weeks, it is likely that you are still getting some gluten in your diet. This could be by accident or simply because you are finding it hard to go without some favourite foods. However, if you feel sure that you are following your diet carefully, do speak to your doctor.

Your dietician will be able to advise you about the need for any vitamin and mineral supplements, together with any other dietary changes that might be necessary: for example, if you also have lactose intolerance (see page 36). Remember, once you start the gluten-free diet, the bowel heals and can start to absorb food and nutrients properly, and problems like lactose intolerance typically resolve.

Most people with coeliac disease soon regain any lost weight once they start a gluten-free diet.

HAVE REGULAR CHECK-UPS

In the first year of diagnosis, it is sensible to have three or four check-ups with your doctor and, whenever possible, your dietician. It helps if close family members visit at some point too, so that they also understand the importance and practicalities of the gluten-free diet. Thereafter, you should aim to have check-ups once or twice a year, just to make sure you are staying well and are still following your diet carefully.

Symptoms may flare up in times of stress or change – pregnancy is a common time for women (see page 27) – so seek regular help and advice from your doctor and dietician at these times.

How to ensure your diet is gluten-free

Hidden ingredients

On food labels, the following ingredients may contain gluten:

- Barley, pot or Scotch barley
- Bran
- Breadcrumbs
- Bulgar or cracked wheat
- Cereal extract
- Couscous
- Cracker meal
- Farina
- Flour, wholemeal flour, wheat flour
- Gluten
- Modified starch
- Rolled oats, oatmeal, porridge oats
- Rusk
- Rye flour
- Semolina
- Spelt, kamut
- Vegetable protein, vegetable gum, vegetable starch
- Wheat bran, wheat germ, wheat starch
- Whole-wheat, wheat

When you have coeliac disease, enjoying a varied gluten-free diet is vital for good health, but it does take practice, vigilance and creativity. You must be extremely careful about what you buy for lunch at school or work, what you eat at dinner parties or in restaurants, and what you do when you feel hungry, either at home or when you are out.

As you will see from the table opposite, most of our basic foods, such as meat, fish, eggs, vegetables, fruit and dairy products, are naturally gluten-free. Gluten is found only in wheat, barley, rye and possibly oats. So following a gluten-free diet means knowing how to avoid everything that contains these grains and their products, notably flour. Wheat flour is the richest and most common source of gluten. The table also shows that as well as occurring in obvious sources such as bread, pasta and biscuits, it is used in many processed foods, often in different guises, making them 'hidden' sources of gluten. For example, some gluten-containing ingredients do not contain the word 'wheat' (see left), labelling laws can mean that not all ingredients actually appear on the food label and there are huge challenges in eating out and away from home (see page 41).

Even if you feel quite well after eating gluten, it could still have affected the bowel, so even though it is understandably tempting to 'break the rules', do try to resist for your health's sake. Be sure to take official gluten-free food directories on shopping trips, look for 'gluten-free' symbols on foods and read labels carefully. The good news is that special pens that test for the presence of gluten are currently being developed and should help to increase food choices and prevent mistakes.

BEWARE CONTAMINATION

As well as avoiding all the obvious sources, it is important to ensure that your gluten-free foods are not 'contaminated' by others that contain gluten. For example, shop-bought meringues and other gluten-free delights are likely to have come into contact with gluten-containing cakes, while chips from a fish and chip shop may have had a meeting with batter in the deep-fat fryer. Also, remember that you should never share breadboards, toasters or butter dishes with users of standard bread.

When eating out, it is vital to check that foods are gluten-free.

Choosing gluten-free foods

Food type	Foods allowed	Foods to avoid/check
Cereals/grains	Maize, all types of rice, sorghum, sago, millet, tapioca, buckwheat, teff, quinoa, rice bran	Wheat, barley, rye, spelt, triticale, kamut, bulgar wheat, couscous, durum wheat, semolina, wheat bran, oats,* oat bran*
Flours	Rice, corn, soya, potato, chestnut, maize, gram, chick pea/channa, sorghum, tapioca	All types of wheat, rye and oat* flour
Breakfast cereals	Any made from permitted cereals	Any made using wheat, rye, barley, oats*
Baked foods, pasta	Gluten-free breads, biscuits, crispbreads, cakes, pastries, flour mix, pasta	Conventional breads, cakes, biscuits, rusks pastries, crispbreads, pasta, ice-cream cones
Meat, poultry, fish and eggs	All plain-cooked varieties and when used in dishes/products with gluten-free ingredients	Savoury pies, pasties, sausages, crumbed, battered, stuffed and processed products
Milk and milk products; soya	Milk, most yogurts, cream, most cheeses; soya milks, yogurts and cheeses; tofu	Yogurt with crunchy ingredients; some artificial creams and processed cheeses
Fats	Butter, margarine, oils, lard, dripping	Suet, some brands of low-fat spread
Vegetables	All types: fresh, frozen, dried, juiced (check ingredients if canned or in ready-made salads or bean and vegetable dishes)	Vegetables in sauce or dressing made using wheat flour; crumbed or battered vegetables; potato waffles and croquettes
Fruit	All types: fresh, frozen, dried, juiced, canned	Some fruit-pie fillings
Soups, sauces	All types thickened/made with gluten-free ingredients; some canned and dried soups	Gravy mixes, soups and sauces made with non-permitted flour or pasta
Desserts	Jelly, milk or soya desserts made from gluten-free cereals; some ice creams, sorbets and mousses	Desserts made using wheat flour, semolina, breadcrumbs, oats* or suet
Snack foods	Plain nuts and seeds, some brands of crisps, savoury snacks, dips, sweets and chocolates	Sweet and savoury snacks made using non-permitted flours, liquorice
Drinks	Wine, spirits, liqueurs, cider; tea, pure coffee, cocoa, fizzy drinks, juices, most squashes and soft drinks	Real ales, beer, lager, stout; coffee or other drinks containing barley, malted drinks, vending-machine drinks
Miscellaneous	Pure salt, pepper, herbs, spices, vinegar, bicarbonate of soda, cream of tartar; some brands of mixed spices, curry powder, baking powder, yeast, essences, dressings; honey, jams, marmalade, molasses, nut butters	Spices, baking powders, dressings or any other ingredients containing wheat, rye, barley or oats; some medicines and vitamins; spreads containing wheat flour

* Research now suggests that some people with coeliac disease can safely eat moderate amounts of oats (see page 18), but check with your doctor or dietician before including them in your diet.

Following a wheat-free diet

Ingredients to avoid

- Bran, wheat bran, wheat germ
- Cereal filler, cereal binder, cereal protein
- Farina
- Flour, wholemeal flour, wheat flour, wheat starch
- Rusk
- Starch, modified starch, edible starch
- Vegetable protein, vegetable gum, vegetable starch
- Wheat, durum wheat, semolina, couscous, bulgar/cracked wheat, spelt

Adults and children with a medically diagnosed wheat allergy or wheat intolerance will need to follow a diet that excludes wheat and all foods containing wheat flour and wheat-derived ingredients. However, unlike coeliac disease, which is a lifelong condition, wheat allergy or intolerance may be transient. For example, young children may 'grow out' of wheat allergy by school-age. If you or your child suffers from wheat intolerance, it is always worth retrying wheat every six months or so. (See page 11.)

DIAGNOSING WHEAT INTOLERANCE

As the symptoms of wheat intolerance and coeliac disease are often very similar, such as bowel upsets, tiredness and bloating, it can be difficult to tell them apart. Also, if people with either condition cut wheat from their diet, they are likely to feel better (see page 10).

A WHEAT-FREE DIET

Unlike a gluten-free diet, a wheat-free diet can include rye, barley and oats. This means the diet can be varied with rye bread and crackers, barley in soups and casseroles, oat cakes and porridge. Note, though, that specially manufactured gluten-free foods such as flour mixes and pasta may be made from deglutenized wheat, making them unsuitable for wheat-free diets.

Wheat is also 'hidden' in many foods, so you need to look out for hidden ingredients when you are shopping or eating away from home:

- Always read ingredients lists on food labels.
- Check processed foods in wheat-free food guides supplied by supermarkets.
- Avoid contamination from breadboards, toasters and bakeries.
- When eating away from home, always check that ingredients are wheat-free (in advance if possible); if there is any doubt, avoid them.
- Take wheat-free bread, meals or snacks with you if you are unsure about availability.
- Use this book, collect other recipes and make use of information from wheat-free food manufacturers.
- Seek your dietician's advice to ensure nutritional adequacy and to help you recheck whether your wheat intolerance still exists.

Pure rye breads and crackers are suitable for a wheat-free diet.

Gluten-free foods

To help make gluten-free diets more varied, specially manufactured gluten-free products made from gluten-free ingredients have been developed by different food companies. These include bread, biscuits, cakes, flour mixes, breakfast cereals and pasta. The companies also provide recipe ideas, free samples and general information about living with coeliac disease and following a gluten-free diet. The products can be bought from supermarkets and health food stores, by mail order and via internet shopping. A number of everyday products, such as bread, pasta and biscuits, are available on prescription. Check with your doctor or dietician for more details.

You may see products described as either 'wheat starch/gluten-free' or 'wheat-free/gluten-free'. This is because 'wheat starch/gluten-free' products are based on wheat starch developed to the worldwide standards set by Codex Alimentarius (an organization established by the World Health Organization and Food and Agriculture Organization), and so has gluten removed to a level that is normally associated with not causing damage to the intestine. Unlike 'wheat-free/gluten-free' products, they are not suitable for wheat-free diets, but both types are suitable for people suffering from coeliac disease.

Specially-manufactured gluten-free foods help make a gluten-free diet more varied.

Moderate amounts of oats may be suitable for some people with coeliac disease – check with your doctor.

FREQUENTLY ASKED QUESTIONS

It can be hard to know if certain items are gluten-free or not. These include alcoholic drinks, especially since in some countries their ingredients do not need to be listed on the labels. It is also possible that gluten-containing food-processing aids, fillers or ingredient 'carriers' have been used and, quite legally, do not appear on the labels. This is why it is vital to go shopping with official gluten-free food guides from national coeliac societies, to look for gluten-free symbols on foods and, when in doubt, to leave it out.

What about oats?

Until recently, oats had always been avoided on a gluten-free diet, but now doctors in some countries do permit them in certain circumstances. Oats contain proteins similar to gliadin (the problematic part of gluten), but in much smaller amounts than wheat, barley and rye. A number of research studies have shown that most people with coeliac disease can safely eat moderate amounts of oats. One potential problem, however, is that during processing, oats may be contaminated with gluten from wheat products processed in the same factory. Also, since some people react much more strongly to gluten than others, even the small amounts of the proteins found in oats may be problematic for them. The safest approach is to assume that oats are off your menu, unless your doctor has advised otherwise.

What about drugs, medicines and supplements?

It is possible that these contain gluten in some form, so it is wise to check with your doctor and/or pharmacist before taking prescriptions or over-the-counter medications, or if you seem to be getting bad reactions to medicines you are already taking. In the case of supplements you buy yourself, you may need to contact the manufacturer directly.

What about postage stamps?

As a general rule, the gum used on postage stamps is gluten-free, but you may want to double-check with your post office, or use self-adhesive ones.

Can I eat communion wafers?

Most communion wafers are not gluten-free and just one can be enough to trigger symptoms. However, your local coeliac society or official food directory will give advice on how to buy gluten-free versions.

Is it safe for children to use paints and doughs for play?

Modelling doughs, paints and glues are not gluten-free, so make sure children with coeliac disease do not put them in their mouths.

Can I eat malt and malt extract?

Malt comes from barley and pure malt extract and malted drinks must be avoided on a gluten-free diet. Malt extract and malt-extract flavourings are widely used in foods and are unlikely to be problematic in the very small amounts normally consumed. The best advice, as ever, is to keep to only those processed foods listed in official gluten-free guides and those labelled as gluten-free.

Which alcoholic drinks are suitable?

Gluten-free drinks include all wines, champagnes, ciders, perries, spirits (including malt whisky), liqueurs, ports, vermouths and sherries. However, all beers, lagers, real ales and stouts must be avoided.

Are modified starch and maltodextrin gluten-free?

Modified starch could be gluten-free if the starch comes from potato, maize, rice or tapioca. However, unless this information appears on the food label, it could be made from wheat, barley or rye, in which case it would not be gluten-free. The word 'modified' refers to the fact that the starch has been processed to make it thicken foods better; it has not been genetically modified or modified to remove its gluten content. Maltodextrin, on the other hand, is gluten-free.

Is it OK to touch gluten-containing foods or cosmetics?

Touching products which contain gluten will not cause an adverse reaction as gluten is only a problem if it is eaten or breathed in. It is important, therefore, to always use gluten-free flour when cooking so that if you inhale any, it won't cause an adverse reaction.

Not all alcoholic drinks are gluten-free, so check gluten-free guides.

Choosing a balanced diet

Enjoying a balanced diet is important for everyone and that, of course, includes people following a gluten-free diet. Good food does more than simply taste good; it nourishes both body and spirit, helping us to stay bright and alert, to fight infection and to generate the energy we need to keep getting the best from life. It also helps reduce the risk of many common health problems, such as obesity, heart disease, osteoporosis and cancers.

A balanced diet should include a selection from all of the five food groups listed in the table that follows. This is only a general guide and is not meant for children under five, who have different dietary needs (see page 24–25). To ensure that the processed foods you choose are gluten-free, read all labels carefully and/or check to see if they are listed in official gluten-free food directories from national coeliac societies.

	Main nutrients	What to choose	How much	Other points
Potatoes, rice, gluten-free breads, cereals, pasta and other grains 	Carbohydrate • fibre • B vitamins • potassium • some protein • iron • vitamin E • calcium • phytochemicals*	Rice • potatoes • yams • gluten-free bread and crackers, rice and corn cakes • gluten-free pasta, noodles, breakfast cereals • other gluten-free grains	**5–11 portions daily** One portion: 1 slice of bread 1 bowl of cereal 3 crispbreads 100 g (3½ oz) cooked rice pasta or noodles	People with coeliac disease may be tempted to limit these foods in their diet, but they are a nutritious part of a balanced diet.
Fruit and vegetables 	Vitamin C • folic acid • beta-carotene • fibre • magnesium • potassium • some carbohydrate • iron • calcium • phytochemicals*	All types: fresh, frozen, canned, dried • juices	**5–9 portions daily** One portion: a medium fruit 2–3 tablespoons vegetables glass of juice 1 tablespoon dried fruit	Diets rich in fruit and vegetables can help protect against long-term diseases and help weight-control.

	Main nutrients	What to choose	How much	Other points
Milk and dairy foods, and alternatives 	Calcium • protein • vitamins B2, B12, A and D • zinc • phytochemicals* in soya-based foods	Lower-fat varieties such as reduced-fat milks, yogurt, fromage frais and cheeses • calcium-fortified soya milk or yogurt	**2–3 portions daily** One portion: 200 ml (7 fl oz) milk small pot yogurt 30 g (1¼ oz) cheese 100 g (3½ oz) cottage cheese	A good calcium intake throughout life (especially during adolescence and the early twenties) helps to reduce the risk of osteoporosis.
Meat, fish and alternatives 	Protein • iron • B vitamins • zinc • magnesium • potassium • phytochemicals* in peas, beans, lentils, nuts, seeds, tofu	Lean and trimmed meats • poultry • fish • eggs • beans • split peas • lentils • nuts • meat substitutes	**2–3 portions daily** One portion: 100 g (3½ oz) meat 150 g (5 oz) fish 1–2 eggs 4–5 tablespoons cooked beans	Important to help prevent anaemia. Include 1 portion of oily fish (trout, salmon, mackerel or sardines) each week.
Foods rich in fat and/or sugar	Fat, including some essential fats • vitamins • minerals and sugars • phytochemicals* in virgin olive oil, sesame oil and chocolate	Unsaturated oils such as olive, rapeseed, groundnut, soya and their spreads • lower-fat dressings and ready meals. Nuts make a good snack.	Eat in small amounts, especially foods high in saturated fat. Check labels carefully to ensure products are gluten-free.	Use fats sparingly when preparing food. A high intake of saturated fats is linked to increased risk of heart disease. Keep sugary foods and drinks to mealtimes to reduce the risk of tooth decay.

* Phytochemicals are natural compounds found in fruit, vegetables, pulses, brown rice, buckwheat, millet, nuts and seeds. They give plants their distinct taste, texture and colours. They are not true nutrients but seem to protect our health in different ways. Some block the development of cancer cells, others influence chemical reactions that regulate body functions and many work as antioxidants. They help to explain why greens are so good for us!

Salt, alcohol and fluid

SALT

Everybody needs a little salt, but it is important to watch your intake, especially if you suffer from high blood pressure. A liking for salt is very much down to habit and if you cut down gradually your tastebuds will adjust. Try these tips to help you keep to the recommended limit of 6 g a day.

● Around three-quarters of the salt we eat comes from processed foods, so cook with fresh ingredients whenever possible.

● Look out for salt-reduced canned and packaged foods.

● Limit or skip adding salt when cooking or at the table.

● Use herbs, spices, garlic, wine, lemon juice, vinegar and tomato purée to add natural flavour to cooking.

● Salt usually appears as sodium chloride on food labels. To convert to grams of salt, multiply the sodium value by 2.5. So, for example, 2.2 g sodium will give you 5.5 g salt.

ALCOHOL

Most of us like to enjoy a drink but keep in mind 'sensible' limits, which are set to protect our health. The current daily recommended limits are 2–3 units for women and 3–4 units for men. A unit contains 8 g of alcohol and is equivalent to:

● half a pint (285 ml) of standard cider

● small glass of wine or champagne

● 25 ml spirits

● 50 ml glass of sherry or port.

All of these drinks are suitable on a gluten-free diet.

DRINK ENOUGH FLUID

Around two-thirds of the body is made up of fluid. This is constantly lost when we sweat and breathe, as well as in urine and bowel motions. To replace these losses most people need to drink at least 1.5 litres (6–8 glasses) of fluid each day. More is needed in hot weather and/or if you are exercising. The best way to check that you are drinking enough is to note the colour of your urine. It should be a light straw colour; if it is dark, then you need to drink more.

It is important to drink plenty of fluids every day.

Healthy gluten-free cooking

FRIDGE AND STORE CUPBOARD ESSENTIALS

Stock your fridge with fish, chicken, eggs, lean meat, a range of dairy foods, fruit and fresh or frozen vegetables. Also make sure that you have a variety of gluten-free basics in your store cupboard ready for quick, nutritious meal and snack preparation (always double-check branded processed foods with your official gluten-free food guide). Take time to experiment with new ingredients and gluten-free grains, and to adapt favourite recipes. Most ingredients can be bought from supermarkets but visit health foods shops and speciality internet sites too if you want to try more exotic items.

Essential store cupboard items

- Canned or dried beans, peas, lentils
- Gluten-free breakfast cereals, millet flakes
- Corn crispbread, rice cakes
- Canned salmon, mackerel, sardines, tuna
- Rice, corn and gluten-free pasta and noodles
- Different types of rice – try basmati, jasmine, wild or red rice
- Buckwheat, millet, tapioca, sago
- Canned tomatoes, passata, sweetcorn, new potatoes
- Popping corn, plain nuts, seeds
- Dried apricots, figs, raisins, sultanas
- Canned tropical fruit and berries
- Lemon and lime juice, salad dressings, flavoured vinegars, garlic, onion, ginger, chilli, other herbs and spices, soy sauce, hot sauce, capers, olives, wine, tomato paste, mustard – make sure these are gluten-free
- Olive, rapeseed, sesame, walnut or chilli oil

COOKING TIP

Xanthan gum is gluten-free and becomes 'stretchy' when wet. This means it makes bread, cakes and pastry softer, with a less crumbly texture. Simply mix in 1 teaspoon of xanthan gum per 125 g/4 oz of gluten-free flour before adding wet ingredients as per your recipe.

Healthy cooking equipment

- Steamer
- Nonstick pans
- Barbecue
- Wok
- Food processor
- Pressure cooker
- Skillet
- Oil spray
- Natural bristle brush
- Vegetable scrubber and peeler

Stock your store cupboard with healthy gluten-free ingredients, such as dried fruit.

Gluten-free eating for different ages

BABIES AND YOUNG CHILDREN

If babies or toddlers are going to develop coeliac disease, it usually happens between the ages of nine months and three years. Both breast milk and infant formula are gluten-free, so a baby's predisposition to coeliac disease will not appear until weaning starts. All mothers – including those with coeliac disease – are encouraged to breast-feed for at least four months, if possible, and advised to start weaning from four months of age – and then with gluten-free foods (see opposite). This is especially important if coeliac disease runs in the

All parents are encouraged to wean their baby on gluten-free foods.

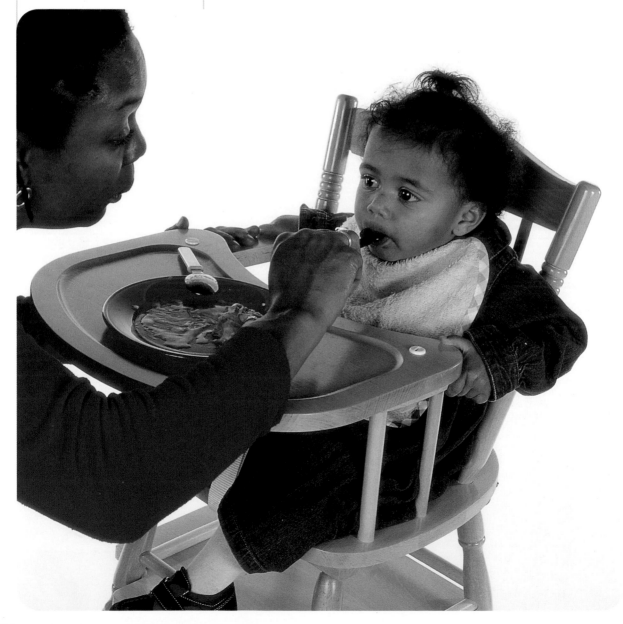

family. If your baby is healthy, gluten-containing foods such as wheat-based cereals, bread and pasta can be gradually introduced from six months, as part of a normal infant's diet. Since your baby will be stronger at this age, if he or she is going to develop coeliac disease it is best to let it happen clearly, to allow for easier diagnosis (see page 9). Once it has been diagnosed, all sources of gluten must be strictly excluded from the diet.

Expert dietary advice from a dietician is essential to ensure that your baby gets the nutrition necessary for growth and development. Once the gluten-free diet starts, he or she will gradually return to being a happy, healthy child. Regular check-ups with the doctor and dietician are essential. It can also be helpful to meet with other parents who have young children with coeliac disease to share experiences and support.

Make sure your child's dietary needs are catered for at events away from home, such as birthday parties.

Feeding babies and young children

- Breast milk or infant formula for first year
- Weaning starts between four and six months – suitable first foods include puréed or mashed potato, carrot, parsnip, ripe banana, avocado, apple, pear, gluten-free cereal
- Avoid gluten until six months
- Iron and vitamin C-rich foods from six months (see page 29)
- Use full-fat dairy foods and spreads
- Varied meals by the end of the first year – gluten-free if they have coeliac disease

Feeding young children with coeliac disease

- Three family-type gluten-free meals, plus snacks such as gluten-free toast, yogurt, fruit, vegetable sticks, fruit shakes, to suit appetite
- Two or three servings of calcium-rich foods such as full-fat milk, follow-on milk, gluten-free cheese sauce, yogurt, cheese, fromage frais
- Vitamin D from food and some gentle sunlight (see page 30)
- Iron and vitamin C-rich foods (see page 29)
- If children are away from home, make sure carers understand the gluten-free diet

Packed lunches are the best option if a gluten-free lunch at school can't be ensured.

SCHOOL-AGE CHILDREN

Once children get close to school age they will be aware that there is something different about them, so it is best to talk openly and positively about their coeliac disease and gluten-free diet, both to them and to others. Educating your child (and any carers) about a gluten-free diet is vital too, so he or she will be able to manage at school, birthday parties or any meal away from home. Schools should be able to provide gluten-free meals, but if not, a packed lunch is the best option.

Children use a lot of energy – they are growing and developing, they rush around playing – so they need nourishing food for fuel. Early experience of food will also help shape their eating habits in later life. By continuing to be a good role model, parents can encourage children to enjoy and experience a wide variety of tasty and nourishing gluten-free foods, as well as help them to understand why their diet is different. Relaxed family meals away from the television and other distractions, and with shared gluten-free dishes, helps to develop the social side and positive pleasures of food too.

Make sure you and your child see the dietician regularly for individualized advice about nutritional needs. If your child was very unwell before diagnosis, he or she may struggle to enjoy food at all. Regular contact helps to ensure that the diet is strictly followed and can also reassure parents that they are right not to give their children gluten-containing 'treats' – which are no doubt asked for.

TEENAGE YEARS

Around 95 per cent of the maximum strength of the skeleton is laid down by late teens. More protein, calcium and zinc are needed to help build new tissue, muscle and bone, and menstruation means girls' iron requirements almost double. Meanwhile, busy social lives can lead to skipped meals or convenience food on the run. Body-image concerns are common, as is experimentation with food fads.

Having to follow a gluten-free diet on top of all this can make things tricky. Teenagers are likely to need extra help and advice about eating out safely and choosing suitable alcoholic drinks. Hungry boys, in particular, need plenty of gluten-free snacks to reduce the chance of dietary lapses. Following the diet strictly ensures that nutrients are absorbed properly, thus enabling increased nutritional needs to be met. It also helps teenagers to feel well and so reduces the risk of low mood – which can be enough of a problem at that age.

The main thing is for parents and their children to maintain a sense of proportion. While a strict gluten-free diet is very important, the occasional lapse will not ruin everything. Accepting this fact will help everyone manage better during difficult times.

PREGNANCY

Nutrition affects every aspect of our bodily functions, including fertility and pregnancy. A baby develops rapidly during the first six to eight weeks, and women may not realize they are pregnant for a lot of this time. This means it is important for women, and men too, to be well nourished before they start trying for a baby. Sadly, untreated coeliac disease in either partner increases the risk of infertility or miscarriage, but people with well-managed coeliac disease can look forward to a healthy pregnancy.

It is recommended that all women planning pregnancy (and then for the first 12 weeks of pregnancy) should take a daily 400 microgram folic acid supplement to reduce the risk of neural tube defects such as spina bifida. Eating more foods rich in folic acid is also advisable (see page 20), and research suggests that good intakes of all B vitamins, zinc, magnesium and calcium are important for the baby's health.

If you have recently been diagnosed with coeliac disease or are not confident that your diet is well balanced, it makes sense to take a multi-vitamin and mineral supplement. Make sure its nutrients do not exceed the recommended daily amounts, as high doses of nutrients such as vitamin A may adversely affect the baby (note that liver is very high in vitamin A, so it must be avoided during pregnancy). Supplements designed for pregnancy are a good choice, but if you are unsure speak to your doctor, dietician or pharmacist.

A balanced diet

At your first antenatal check, make sure the relevant people know you have coeliac disease. Pregnancy does not mean having to 'eat for two' (you need to increase your calorie intake by just 200 a day, and then only in the last three months), but the quality of your diet is important. Keeping strictly to your balanced gluten-free diet will optimize nutrient absorption and minimize any risk of problems such as anaemia.

Foods rich in omega-3 fats – oily fish, walnuts, rapeseed oil, pumpkin seeds and omega-3 enriched eggs – are important for the baby's developing brain, retina and nervous system. Vitamin D is needed to absorb and use calcium properly, so supplements may be advised for pregnant and breast-feeding women with limited exposure to sunlight.

Breast-feeding

Breast milk provides the optimal balance of nutrients for growth and development, as well as antibodies to build up immunity. Infant formula is available for mothers who are unable or choose not to breast-feed. Nutrient needs increase more during breast-feeding than pregnancy, especially for calcium, magnesium, zinc and vitamin C (see page 20). On average, breast-feeding women need an extra 500 calories a day, so this can be wisely 'spent' on extra low-fat dairy foods, fish, fruit and vegetables.

Foods rich in omega-3 fats, such as oily fish and walnuts, are important during pregnancy.

ELDERLY PEOPLE

Coeliac disease can arrive at any time of life. About 20 per cent of people diagnosed with the condition are over 60 and some are even over 80. If people have other health problems or just feel that they are suffering from 'old age', the danger is that their symptoms will be overlooked.

Good nutrition is vital throughout life to keep the immune system strong and to maintain health and well-being. With age, calorie needs usually decline, but some vitamin and mineral needs increase as the body uses or absorbs them less efficiently. Real problems can start if people are not following their gluten-free diet properly or interest in food wanes because of poor appetite, a limited budget, loneliness, illness or medication. A once-a-day multivitamin and mineral supplement is prudent for people over 65, while a weekly check on weight will flag up unhealthy weight loss, which is a sign that extra medical and nutritional help may be needed.

Coeliac disease affects people of all ages and good nutrition is important throughout life.

Anaemia

Around 80 per cent of people diagnosed with coeliac disease are anaemic. In this case, anaemia develops because the body is unable to properly absorb key nutrients, such as iron which is needed to make the haemoglobin found in healthy red blood cells. While iron-deficiency anaemia is the most common type, a lack of folic acid or vitamin B12 cause a different type of anaemia.

Symptoms of anaemia include tiredness, feeling irritable, lack of appetite, lower resistance to infection and breathlessness. In children, it can also affect development and performance at school.

If you are anaemic, when diagnosed your doctor may prescribe supplements, and your dietician will advise on how to include iron-rich foods in your gluten-free diet. Strictly following your gluten-free diet is vital, as it allows your body to absorb iron and other nutrients properly.

Preventing anaemia

- Good sources of iron include liver, red meat, oily fish, shellfish, beans and lentils, iron-fortified gluten-free breakfast cereals, poultry, green vegetables, nuts, dried fruit and gluten-free bread.
- The iron found in foods of animal origin is absorbed much better than iron from non-meat sources such as pulses, gluten-free cereals, nuts and green vegetables.
- Vitamin C-rich fruit, vegetables or juices with meals boosts iron absorption from non-meat foods. This is especially important for vegetarians (see page 34).
- Coffee and especially tea can reduce iron absorption. Teenage girls and women of child-bearing age, who are at higher risk of iron deficiency, should aim to drink tea between rather than with meals.

Vitamin C-rich foods help the body absorb iron from non-meat foods.

BABIES' IRON REQUIREMENTS

By six months of age, babies' natural iron stores have run out, so they need iron-rich foods in their daily diet: for example, red meat and iron-fortified gluten-free baby cereals or pulses of a suitable consistency, prepared without added salt or sugar. Breast milk or infant formula – around 600 ml (1 pint) per day – should be their main drink until babies are a year old. Full-fat cows' milk can then be introduced as part of their balanced diet.

Calcium and bone health

Dairy foods are an important source of bone-building calcium.

Bones are made up of a network of fibres packed with bone crystals. These crystals are rich in calcium and other minerals that give bones their strength and 'density'. Osteoporosis develops when bones have lost so much of their mineral content that they become brittle and break easily. People with coeliac disease must take special care to protect themselves from osteoporosis, because they may not absorb calcium and other nutrients as well as they should. Studies suggest that up to 50 per cent of people with coeliac disease may have low bone density. Fortunately, research shows that once children are on a gluten-free diet, bone density improves.

As we have already seen, most of our bone strength is achieved by late teens. However, bones continue to develop until the age of about 25, and from 35 they gradually thin. Hormonal changes at the menopause also increase bone density loss in women. In addition to coeliac disease, too little calcium when young, inactivity, smoking, corticosteroid drugs for asthma, early menopause, eating disorders and a family history of the condition increase the risk of osteoporosis. Talk to your doctor if any of these apply to you. If necessary, you can have a bone scan to assess your bone density.

FEED YOUR BONES

● Enjoy a balanced diet, as a wide range of nutrients – not just calcium – is needed for healthy bones.

● Get enough calcium: choose two or three servings of dairy foods daily (low-fat types are still rich in calcium), plus other good sources such as greens, pulses, fortified gluten-free bread and canned fish with bones (see opposite). Your doctor or dietician may also advise a supplement.

● Get enough vitamin D, which controls calcium absorption. Most comes from the action of gentle sunlight on the skin. Food sources include oily fish, eggs, cheese and fortified foods such as gluten-free cereals and margarine. Daily supplements (no more than 10 micrograms) may be advisable for people over 65, women who are pregnant during the winter, those whose skin is always covered and house-bound people.

● Eat at least five portions of fruit and vegetables daily (see page 20). Diets high in the minerals potassium and magnesium, from fruit and vegetables, are linked to stronger bones in later life.

● If you smoke, aim to stop. Keep to sensible drinking limits (see page 22).

● Note that many specially manufactured gluten-free products are fortified with calcium and contain higher levels than their gluten-containing versions.

Calcium Guide

Food	Calcium content (mg)
Canned sardines with bones (100 g/3½ oz)	460
200 ml/7 fl oz glass whole/semi-skimmed/skimmed milk	237/248/249
Semi-skimmed milk in a mug of tea/coffee	50
200 ml/7 fl oz calcium-fortified orange juice/soya milk	245/240
Piece of hard cheese (30 g/1¼ oz)	216
1 tablespoon grated Cheddar cheese (10 g/⅓ oz)	72
Small pot cottage cheese (125 g/4 oz)	82
Small pot low-fat fruit yogurt (150 g/5 oz)	225
Small pot fruit fromage frais (100 g/3½ oz)	86
Small pot low-fat rice pudding (150 g/5 oz)	140
2 slices white/wholemeal bread	66/33
Portion of broccoli/cabbage	36
Small can baked beans (150 g/5 oz)	80
Shelled prawns (60 g/2⅓ oz)	90
1 orange	72
2 dried figs	50

EXERCISE YOUR BONES

● Stay active with weekly weight-bearing exercise: for example, brisk walking, aerobics, skipping, dancing and resistance training to put stress on bones.

● Just move more often. Regular activity improves balance, coordination, flexibility and muscle strength, which in turn help to reduce the risk of falling and breaking a bone.

Regular exercise puts stress on bones, helping to keep them strong.

Weight control

Weight loss is a common symptom of untreated coeliac disease. Once they start their gluten-free diet, however, most people gradually regain the lost weight. If you find that this does not happen, then contact your dietician. It may be that you are unwittingly eating gluten, or simply that you do not eat enough and would benefit from some healthy, calorie-boosting additions to your diet. All children should see their doctor and dietician regularly (see pages 24–27) to ensure that their weight, height and general development are progressing normally.

WATCHING YOUR WEIGHT

Being overweight rather than underweight is a more common problem for people with treated coeliac disease. No doubt this is at least in part the result of feeling well and enjoying food again once your condition has been diagnosed. It is also not surprising when you consider that over half of all adults are overweight. Being overweight can affect health in many ways. It increases the risk of Type 2 diabetes, heart disease, high blood pressure, back and joint pain, infertility and certain cancers, so it is not just a cosmetic issue.

The calories we consume (food and drink) and the calories we burn (metabolism and activity) largely determine body weight. To keep weight stable these must be in balance and to lose weight you must take in fewer calories than you burn. These days most people in the West need to take care to eat wisely and stay active as we are all being constantly beset by tempting food at a time when labour-saving devices mean less and less energy-expending activity is needed.

To lose weight at a healthy rate of around 500 g (1 lb) a week you need to eat 500 fewer calories than you usually do every day. To do this you do not have to change your diet radically or count calories all the time. Some simple lifestyle changes, taken step by step, can tip the balance in your favour. For example, switching to lower-fat foods and cooking methods, swapping some high-fat snacks for fruit and building in extra daily activity (see opposite) could be enough.

Try to choose healthy snacks, such as fruit, instead of ones which are high in fat or sugar.

Successful slimmers swear by these tips:

- Be realistic about target weights and rate of weight loss: trying to lose too much too quickly can throw you off course.
- Think long-term rather than following rigid or quick-fix diet plans.
- Keep a food and thoughts diary to identify problem areas. This will also help you to stay aware of what and why you eat, make conscious food choices and identify comfort eating or negative thoughts that thwart progress.
- Plan ahead for regular meals and snacks.
- Include at least five portions of fruit and vegetables in your diet every day (see page 20).
- Choose lower-fat foods and use low-fat cooking methods (see right).
- Avoid rigid rules that can lead to 'all or nothing' thinking: for example, 'I have failed by eating that chocolate so I might as well keep on eating.' In this case, it is your reaction, not the chocolate, that is the problem.
- Make a list of distracting activities – for example, going for a walk, phoning a friend, taking a bath – to use when cravings strike. If you do succumb, do not tell yourself off. Instead, put it behind you and plan how to deal with the situation next time.
- Enlist support from a health professional, friend, partner or responsible group. It really does help.

STAY ACTIVE

Being active not only helps you to stay in shape but also decreases your risk of heart disease, contributes to mood and stress management, and is good for your bones. All types of physical activity are beneficial and small changes in day-to-day life can add up to make a real difference. Here are some ideas:

- Use the stairs instead of the lift at work.
- Get off the bus a stop earlier and walk the rest of the way.
- Use the toilet on the next floor up at work.
- Walk or cycle short distances rather than jumping into the car.
- Spend less time sitting or watching TV.
- Build up to 30 minutes (or two 15-minute sessions) of moderate activity at least five times a week. Choose something you enjoy and can incorporate easily into your daily routine: for example, a lunchtime walk, walking the dog, cycling, dancing, aerobics, martial arts, gardening.
- By adding a brisk 30-minute walk to your daily routine you could lose 12 lb (5.5 kg) of fat in a year.

If you are very overweight or have a medical problem, consult your doctor before you make changes to your activity levels.

Healthy cooking tips

- Buy lean meat or trim off any excess fat.
- Grill, bake, microwave, steam, poach, stir-fry or casserole foods instead of frying them. Oil sprays are useful. Roast meat on a rack to allow the fat to drain off.
- Serve baked, mashed, boiled or new potatoes. Oven chips and chunky wedges are better choices than deep-fried chips.
- Low-fat fromage frais and yogurts make tasty alternatives to cream, soured cream or mayonnaise.
- Try using tomato paste, garlic, herbs, spices, olives, vinegar, lemon juice, wine or hot pepper sauces rather than extra fat to flavour food.

Baked potatoes are much healthier than fried and can be served with a variety of toppings.

Vegetarian diets

Pulses are a nutritious alternative to meat in a vegetarian diet.

People choose to become vegetarian for a variety of reasons and a well-balanced vegetarian diet can be health-promoting and enjoyable. However, it is another food restriction on top of the gluten-free diet, so extra care is needed, particularly for those with special nutritional needs: for example, children and teenagers, and pregnant and breast-feeding women. You should see a dietician for the best information about vegetarian diets. This is even more important if you choose to follow a vegan diet, which excludes all animal products, including eggs and dairy foods.

A QUESTION OF BALANCE

When you exclude meat and fish, nutritious alternatives are needed to replace the protein, iron, zinc and B vitamins found in these foods. Pulses (peas, beans and lentils), eggs, tofu, TVP, nuts and seeds are all suitable and are naturally gluten-free.

Milk and dairy foods are important too, but they are from a separate food group (see page 20) and lack iron, so it is not enough to cut out meat and replace it with cheese. If people eat few or no dairy foods, soya milk fortified with calcium and vitamin B12 (B12 is found naturally only in foods of animal origin) should be used daily, along with other calcium-rich foods (see page 31). Dairy foods are also important sources of iodine, which is needed for healthy functioning of the thyroid gland. Other good vegetarian sources are seaweed, iodized salt and fortified yeast extracts.

Gluten-free breads, pastas and cereals, potatoes, rice and other gluten-free grains provide a healthy, filling basis for vegetarian meals and are reasonable iron providers. Standard wholegrain cereals add the mineral selenium to the diet and this may give protection against many long-term diseases, and also regulate mood. Good gluten-free sources include nuts, especially brazil nuts, sunflower seeds and dairy foods. Fish is a rich source too, but is off the menu for vegetarians. Fruit and vegetables are also naturally gluten-free and provide vital vitamin C, which boosts iron absorption from non-meat foods.

FAT MATTERS

Omega-3 fats are vital for a healthy heart, nervous system and immunity, and pregnant women also need them to aid their baby's development (see page 27). Oily fish are the best source, so vegetarians will need to include alternatives such as rapeseed oil, linseeds, walnuts, pumpkin seeds, omega-3-enriched eggs and tofu.

Brazil nuts are rich in the mineral selenium which can be low in a vegetarian diet.

Diabetes

Out of every 25 people with Type 1 (insulin-dependent) diabetes, one will also have coeliac disease, because of a genetic link between the two conditions. This means that both conditions tend to run in families and people with Type 1 diabetes have a greater chance of developing coeliac disease (and vice versa) than the general population. Many experts now recommend that everyone with Type 1 diabetes should be tested for coeliac disease (see page 12), especially those with bowel problems or unexplained anaemia.

Type 1 diabetes usually affects people under 40 and, like coeliac disease, is a lifelong condition. People with untreated Type 1 diabetes have too much sugar (glucose) in the blood. This is because their body stops producing insulin, a hormone that regulates blood glucose levels. The main symptoms of untreated diabetes are thirst, frequent trips to the toilet (day and night), extreme tiredness, weight loss and blurred vision.

Type 1 diabetes is treated with insulin injections, a healthy diet and regular activity. Appropriate treatment reduces the risk of long-term complications such as heart disease and eye, kidney and nerve problems. Your diabetes team will give you personal advice about all of these, but here are some general pointers:

- Eat regular meals and snacks based on starchy foods such as rice, potatoes, pulses, gluten-free bread, cereals, pasta and crackers, fruit or yogurt.
- Aim for at least five portions of fruit, vegetables and pulses each day (see page 20). They are brimming with vitamins and fibre, as well as protective antioxidants, which help to keep the circulation healthy.
- Cut down on fat, especially saturated fat, which can raise cholesterol levels. This is found in fatty meats, full-fat dairy foods, butter, cream and gluten-free cakes and biscuits.
- Put a limit on sugar, especially sugary drinks, since too much can raise blood glucose too quickly, making levels difficult to control.
- Keep to sensible salt and alcohol limits (see page 22).
- Enjoy one portion of oily fish such as canned salmon, sardines, mackerel, pilchards or trout each week. They provide omega-3 fats, which are especially good for heart health.

People with diabetes are advised to have regular meals and snacks based on starchy foods.

Lactose intolerance

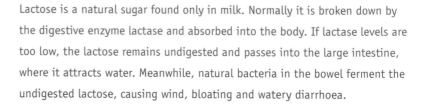

Foods containing lactose

- Milk – all types
- Goats' and sheep's milk
- Milk powder, milk solids
- Buttermilk
- Cheese, cheese powder, cheese flavour
- Yogurt, live yogurt
- Fromage frais
- Butter, margarine (unless it's milk-free)
- Cream/artificial cream
- Ice cream
- Milk sugar
- Milk chocolate
- Lactose
- Hydrolyzed casein
- Whey/whey protein/whey syrup sweetener

Lactose is a natural sugar found only in milk. Normally it is broken down by the digestive enzyme lactase and absorbed into the body. If lactase levels are too low, the lactose remains undigested and passes into the large intestine, where it attracts water. Meanwhile, natural bacteria in the bowel ferment the undigested lactose, causing wind, bloating and watery diarrhoea.

LACTOSE INTOLERANCE AND COELIAC DISEASE

Lactose intolerance can be a long-term genetic condition or a temporary problem brought on by a bad attack of gastroenteritis or a flare-up of a health problem that affects the bowel, such as untreated coeliac disease. Once a strict gluten-free diet is started, the lactose intolerance usually resolves itself. For some, however, it remains a chronic problem.

Lactose intolerance is best diagnosed via a controlled food challenge (see page 11). Your doctor may also arrange for a 'breath hydrogen test'. People with coeliac disease are at higher risk of osteoporosis, so they need to ensure a good calcium intake (see page 30). Dairy foods are the richest sources, so if you cannot tolerate them alternatives are vital. You may find you can manage some dairy foods (see left), but if not, be sure to use other rich sources such as calcium-fortified soya milk and orange juice daily.

MANAGING LACTOSE INTOLERANCE

Most people with lactose intolerance can manage some lactose in their diet: for example, up to a glass of milk spread over the day. Research also suggests that lactose intolerance can be improved by gradually increasing the amount of lactose in the diet, since bacteria in the large intestine seem to adapt to break down lactose.

Dairy products with a low lactose content such as hard cheese, butter and bio-yogurts are usually quite well tolerated. Some trial and error will be involved to find what levels suit you. If you are at all unsure, talk to your dietician about it first.

Many people with lactose intolerance can manage some dairy foods in their diet.

Bowel problems

A gluten-free diet means that many cereal foods and wholegrains are no longer on the menu. Since these are important sources of bowel-regulating fibre, many people find that constipation can be a problem. On the other hand, for some people, their bowels remain a bit grumbly and loose after starting a gluten-free diet. If you suffer from either problem, check out these general guidelines. If your problems persist, speak to your doctor and/or dietician.

CONSTIPATION

Increase the fibre content of your diet and make sure you are drinking enough fluid, because fibre needs fluid to bulk up and work properly. Regular exercise and leaving enough time in the morning – or whenever – for a relaxed sit on the toilet also help deal with the problem.

How to boost your fibre intake

● Have regular meals, starting with breakfast.

● Opt for brown rice and potatoes with skins.

● Include at least five portions of fruit and vegetables in your daily diet – fresh, canned, frozen and juiced (see page 20).

● Include baked beans, other beans, lentils and peas regularly in soups, stews, as a vegetable, in salads or as a snack on toast.

● Different nuts and seeds make high-fibre snacks or additions to salads and rice dishes.

● Choose higher-fibre varieties of specially manufactured gluten-free foods.

● Drink at least six to eight glasses or mugs of fluid each day (see page 22).

● Try bio-yogurts or drinks which contain 'live' lactobacillus bacteria regularly (this may help loose bowels as well as constipation).

● Make changes slowly to let your bowel adapt and so avoid excess flatulence.

LOOSE BOWELS

If your bowels still tend to be on the loose side having followed a gluten-free diet for a few months, there are a number of factors to consider. Ask yourself:

● Are you following your gluten-free diet strictly?

● Are you eating too many fibre-rich foods? Pulses, cabbage, sprouts, corn, onions, pips, skins and seeds can be 'windy' or 'irritating' for some.

● Might you have lactose intolerance (see opposite) or another food intolerance?

Starting the day with a high-fibre breakfast helps to keep bowels in good working order.

Menu plans

These menu plans suggest ways to include the recipes in this book in your gluten-free diet. They show just how varied and tasty meals can be for you and the whole family, and also give ideas for meals if you are following additional dietary regimes: for example, a vegetarian or lactose-free diet.

Standard gluten-free

Breakfast
Breakfast cereal bars
Banana

Potato drop scones
Glass of apple juice

Lunch
Toasted open sandwich
Fruit yogurt

Walnut, pear & green leaf salad
Gluten-free crackers
Fresh fruit

Evening meal
Fish cakes with fennel mayonnaise
Green leaf salad
Caramel fruit pudding

Loin of pork with lentils, with new potatoes
Cherry & almond clafoutis

Snacks
Fresh fruit
Lemony polenta cake

Fruited teacake
Fresh fruit

Vegetarian, gluten-free

Breakfast
Breakfast cornbread with eggs
Glass of orange juice

Cranberry, banana & sesame smoothie

Lunch
Lentil & rosemary soup, with Homemade bread

Hummus with crudités and Spicy bread

Evening meal
Roasted vegetable & red bean stew with rice
Sweet pancakes with citrus sauce

Mushroom risotto with salad
Panacotta with blueberry sauce

Snacks
Dried fruit and nuts
Yogurt

Fresh fruit
Lemony glazed shortbread

Lactose-free, gluten-free

Breakfast
Millet, fruit & nut muesli with soya milk and banana

Mango, orange & soya milkshake

Lunch
Chilli rice noodles
Fresh fruit

Potato & onion tortilla, with salad
Fruited teacake

Evening meal
Mediterranean lamb casserole
Summer pudding

Thai coconut chicken, with jasmine rice
Sorbet, fresh mango

Snacks
Soya yogurt
Fresh fruit

Almond macaroons
Fresh fruit

Diabetes, gluten-free

Breakfast
Homemade bread with favourite spread
Glass of orange juice

Spiced apple porridge
Glass of apple juice

Lunch
Chicken & ham soup
Salad
Fresh fruit

Chickpea flatbread
Fruit yogurt

Evening meal
Spiced beef with spinach, with basmati rice
Fruited teacake

Baked trout with pine nuts, with new potatoes and salad
Almond macaroons

Snacks
Fresh fruit
Fruit yogurt

Rice cakes
Fresh fruit

Young children			
Breakfast Spiced apple porridge Diluted fruit juice	**Lunch** Cheese on gluten-free bread Fruit yogurt	**Evening meal** Little cottage pies Favourite vegetables Plain fairy cake	**Snacks** Banana Glass of milk
Crisped rice cereal with milk Diluted fruit juice	Parsnip & fresh ginger soup Potato drop scones	Homemade veggie sausage & beans Sliced fruit	Fruit yogurt Glass of milk

School-age children			
Breakfast Cornflakes with milk Gluten-free toast with peanut butter Glass of juice	**Lunch** Gluten-free sandwiches Packet of plain crisps Fresh fruit	**Evening meal** Potato pizza margherita Salad Rainbow lollies	**Snacks** Corn & bacon muffin Fruit yogurt
Spiced apple porridge Glass of juice	Filled jacket potato Fruited teacake	Sticky chicken drumsticks Oven chips, peas carrots Fruit yogurt	Breakfast cereal bars Mango, orange & soya milkshake

Children's party ideas

Mini gluten-free sandwiches (check all ingredients are gluten-free):
● savoury fillings: cold meat, roast chicken, cheese spread, tuna, egg, hummus, peanut butter, yeast extract
● sweet fillings: banana and honey, jam, dates, sliced strawberries and cream cheese

Mini Potato pizza margheritas

Corn and bacon muffins, cut into quarters

Potato and onion tortilla, cut into cubes

Hummus

Vegetable sticks – sliced peppers, carrots, mushrooms and celery

Cubes of cheese

Sticky chicken drumsticks (better for older children)

Homemade veggie sausages & beans

Baked potatoes

Plain crisps

Fresh fruit – cut into chunks

Fruited teacake

Almond macaroons

Rainbow lollies

Chocolate lover's birthday cake

Flower fairy cakes

Chocolate fudge crisps

Water, diluted juice and well-diluted squash to drink

Menu plans (continued)

Ideas for entertaining

Spiced and salted nuts for a pre-dinner nibble
Spicy fruit and seed bread to serve with dinner

Starters

Parma ham with melon

Millet 'taboulleh'

Chilled gazpacho

Mascarpone, feta & herb pâté – serve with crudités and
gluten-free toast

Toasted open sandwiches

Walnut, pear & green leaf salad

Buckwheat blinis with smoked fish

Parsnip & fresh ginger soup

Main Courses

(serve with potatoes or rice, vegetables or salad)

Summer roast chicken

Thai coconut chicken

Baked trout with pine nuts

Loin of pork with lentils

Mediterranean lamb casserole

Roasted vegetable & red bean stew

Mushroom risotto made with wild mushrooms

Chilli rice noodles

Desserts

Strawberry meringue roulade

Apricot & marzipan tart

Caramel fruit pudding

Fruit salad, served with (gluten-free) vanilla ice cream

Cherry & almond clafoutis

Coffee & almond trifle

Panacotta with blueberry sauce

Eating away from home

You cannot afford to leave eating out to chance. Think carefully about what friends, hotels or restaurants might serve, and what food will be available when you are travelling or out for a busy day. Before long, planning, questioning and bringing along gluten-free foods will become second nature. Catering processes can limit safe choices unless you know the restaurant or bar well. Use these guidelines to help you through the maze:

Italian
● Pasta, bruschetta, minestrone, garlic bread, cheese sauces and fried fish are off the menu.
● Seafood salad, tomato, avocado and mozzarella salad, or melon and Parma ham make good starters.
● Chicken, fish or liver cooked in sauces without flour are the best main-course options.

Indian
● Tikka and tandoori dishes with no sauce, served with salad and rice, are the safest options.
● Most curries are made with catering-pack sauces which may contain wheat flour. Order only where you can be certain no wheat flour has been used.
● Avoid any breads on the menu.

Chinese
● Avoid soy sauce.
● Skip starters unless you can be sure they are not battered, crumbed or thickened with flour.
● Ask for non-thickened stir-fried dishes made without soy sauce and served with rice.

Burger restaurants
● Most burger chains have comprehensive ingredients lists for their products, so ask for a copy.
● Bring your own gluten-free bun.

Checklist
● Always check that food or drink is gluten-free.
● Take gluten-free foods/snacks with you.
● Check that workplaces serve gluten-free meals or provide facilities for storing or preparing your own.
● Remember to tell anyone who is cooking for you that you can't eat gluten.
● Check in advance that a restaurant can confidently provide gluten-free meals (ask them to check ready-prepared food with the catering supplier).
● Check that the meal you want to order is gluten-free – if there is any doubt, do not order it.
● Plan ahead for snacks for a long train, car or plane journey.
● Find out what foods are available in holiday destinations and hotels.

GETTING FURTHER HELP AND INFORMATION

Following a restricted diet of any type can be tricky, and sometimes isolating, especially when it is a lifelong commitment. Sharing knowledge and experiences, and just being able to chat to people who either live with or know about the condition, can be a great help and support. This is equally true for children of all ages as well as adults.

National and local charities and support groups exist in most countries, so find your nearest group and make the most of what it has to offer.

Potato drop scones

Makes 12
Preparation: 10 minutes
Cooking: 20–25 minutes

550 g/1 lb 2 oz large potatoes

1½ teaspoons Gluten-free
   baking powder (see below)

2 medium eggs

75 ml/3 fl oz whole milk

salt and pepper

oil for frying

1 Cut the potatoes into small chunks and cook in boiling, lightly salted water for 15 minutes or until completely tender. Drain well, return to the pan and mash until smooth. Leave to cool slightly.

2 Beat in the baking powder, then the eggs, milk and a little seasoning, and continue to beat until everything is evenly combined.

3 Heat a little oil in a heavy-based frying pan. Drop heaped dessertspoonfuls of the mixture into the pan, spacing them slightly apart, and fry for 3–4 minutes, turning once, until golden. Transfer to a serving plate and keep warm while frying the remainder of the potato mixture. (If grilling the potato scones, put them on an oiled, foil-lined baking sheet and cook under a preheated grill for 5 minutes, turning once halfway through the cooking time.) Serve warm.

Gluten-free baking powder:

125 g/4 oz rice flour

50 g/2 oz bicarbonate of soda

50 g/2 oz tartaric acid

Preparation: 5–10 minutes

1 Mix together all the ingredients and sieve several times. Store the powder in a screw-top jar.

Nutritional information per scone:
Energy: 68 kcals/287 kJ **Protein:** 2 g
Carbohydrate: 8 g **Fat:** 3 g **Fibre:** 1 g
Calcium: 15 mg **Iron:** <1 mg

Millet, fruit & nut muesli

Serves 4
Preparation: 3 minutes
Cooking: 2 minutes

100 g/3½ oz millet flakes

25 g/1 oz chopped mixed nuts

50 g/2 oz sultanas

50 g/2 oz dried apricots,
   prunes or dates, chopped

25 g/1 oz unsweetened
   desiccated coconut

25 g/1 oz sunflower seeds

25 g/1 oz linseeds

1 Put the millet and nuts in a heavy-based frying pan and cook over a gentle heat, stirring frequently, for 2–3 minutes until they begin to colour. Tip them into a bowl and leave to cool for 10 minutes.

2 Add the dried fruits, coconut and seeds and mix together well. Store in a jar or bowl for up to one week. Serve with either milk or fruit juice.

VARIATION:

The quantities of fruit and nuts in this nutritious cereal can be varied or substituted with other ingredients to suit personal taste and preferences.

Nutritional information per serving:
Energy: 289 kcals/1208 kJ **Protein:** 7 g
Carbohydrate: 35 g **Fat:** 14 g **Fibre:** 7 g
Calcium: 42 mg **Iron:** 2 mg

Spiced apple porridge

Serves 1
Preparation: 1 minute
Cooking: 3–4 minutes

225 ml/7½ fl oz apple juice

½ teaspoon ground cinnamon

25 g/1 oz millet flakes

TO SERVE:

Greek yogurt

demerara sugar (optional)

1 Put the apple juice and cinnamon in a heatproof serving bowl. Sprinkle in the millet flakes and stir gently.

2 Microwave on full power for 3–4 minutes, stirring frequently until thick and creamy. Serve with spoonfuls of yogurt and, if you like your porridge sweet, sprinkled with sugar.

VARIATION:

For a change, try using fresh orange juice instead of apple juice, adding a little honey for extra sweetness if necessary.

TIP

To cook the porridge in a saucepan, put the ingredients into a small pan and heat gently, stirring frequently, for 6–8 minutes until thick and creamy. Add a little extra juice if the mixture becomes dry.

Nutritional information per serving:
Energy: 174 kcals/739 kJ **Protein:** 2 g
Carbohydrate: 40 g **Fat:** 1 g **Fibre:** 2 g
Calcium: 50 mg **Iron:** 1 mg

Breakfast cereal bars

Makes 16
Preparation: 10 minutes
Cooking: 25–30 minutes

100 g/3½ oz butter, softened

25 g/1 oz light muscovado sugar

2 tablespoons golden syrup

125 g/4 oz millet flakes

50 g/2 oz quinoa

50 g/2 oz dried cherries or cranberries

75 g/3 oz sultanas

25 g/1 oz sunflower seeds

25 g/1 oz sesame seeds

25 g/1 oz linseeds

40 g/1½ oz unsweetened desiccated coconut

2 eggs, lightly beaten

1 Grease a 28 x 20 cm/11 x 8 inch shallow rectangular baking tin. Beat together the butter, sugar and syrup until creamy.

2 Add all the remaining ingredients and beat well until combined. Turn into the tin and level the surface with the back of a dessertspoon.

3 Bake in a preheated oven, 180°C (350°F), Gas Mark 4, for 35 minutes until deep golden. Leave to cool in the tin.

4 Turn out on to a wooden board and carefully cut into 16 fingers using a serrated knife. Store in an airtight container for up to 5 days.

TIP

These crumbly breakfast bars are a much healthier alternative to shop-bought cereal bars. Not only are they ideal for quick breakfasts, they make great snacks or lunch box fillers, too.

Nutritional information per serving:
Energy: 156 kcals/650 kJ **Protein:** 3 g
Carbohydrate: 16 g **Fat:** 9 g **Fibre:** 1 g
Calcium: 54 mg **Iron:** 1 mg

Homemade bread

Makes 1 small loaf
Preparation: 5 minutes
Cooking: see manual

375 ml/13 fl oz water

1 teaspoon salt

15 g/½ oz butter, melted

1 tablespoon caster sugar

500 g/1 lb gluten-free bread
   mix for bread machines

2 tablespoons sesame seeds

2 tablespoons sunflower seeds

1 tablespoon poppy seeds

1 teaspoon easy-blend dried
   yeast

1 Put all the ingredients into the bread machine bucket, following the order and method given in the manual, and adding the seeds with the flour.

2 Fit the bucket into the machine and set to the programme and crust setting recommended for breads.

3 Once baked, transfer to a wire rack to cool.

Making bread by hand:

Preparation: 5 minutes, plus rising
Cooking: 20–25 minutes

Mix 1½ teaspoons easy-blend dried yeast with 1 tablespoon caster sugar and 225 ml/7½ fl oz tepid water and milk, mixed. Leave for 5 minutes until frothy. Sift 200 g/7 oz brown or white rice flour, 100 g/3½ oz potato flour and 50 g/2 oz cornmeal into a bowl. Add ½ teaspoon salt, 1 beaten egg, 2 tablespoons olive oil and the yeast mixture, then stir to make a smooth, stiff batter.

   Turn into a greased 900 g/2 lb non-stick loaf tin. Secure inside a large polythene bag and leave in a warm place to rise for about 45 minutes or until risen to the top of the tin. Bake in a preheated oven 200°C (400°F), Gas Mark 6, for 20–25 minutes until firm. Transfer to wire rack to cool.

Nutritional information per slice:
Energy: 213 kcals/895 kJ **Protein:** 2 g
Carbohydrate: 43 g **Fat:** 4 g **Fibre:** 3 g
Calcium: 21 mg **Iron:** <1 mg

Breakfast cornbread

Makes 8 slices
Preparation: 5 minutes
Cooking: 25–30 minutes

100 g/3½ oz fine cornmeal

75 g/3 oz chickpea flour

1½ teaspoons Gluten-free
   baking powder (see page 42)

1 egg

25 g/1 oz butter, melted

250 ml/8 fl oz whole or semi-
   skimmed milk

salt and pepper

1 Lightly oil a 500 g/1 lb loaf tin. Put the cornmeal, flour, baking powder and a little salt and pepper in a bowl and make a well in the centre. Beat the egg with the butter and milk and add a little to the bowl.

2 Beat with a whisk, gradually incorporating the dry ingredients to make a smooth paste. Add the remaining milk mixture and whisk until smooth.

3 Turn into the prepared tin and bake in a preheated oven, 170°C (325°F), Gas Mark 3, for 25–30 minutes until just firm. Leave in the tin for 10 minutes, before transfering to a wire rack to cool.

VARIATION:

For a larger loaf, double up on the ingredients and bake in a 1 kg/2 lb loaf tin. Add an extra 10 minutes to the cooking time.

TIP

This quick and easy bread is delicious simply spread with butter or topped with scrambled or poached eggs.

Nutritional information per slice:
Energy: 130 kcals/545 kJ **Protein:** 5 g
Carbohydrate: 15 g **Fat:** 6 g **Fibre:** 1 g
Calcium: 60 mg **Iron:** <1 mg

Cranberry, banana & sesame smoothie

Makes 1 large
or 2 small glasses
Preparation: 2 minutes

40 g/1½ oz dried cranberries

juice of ½ lemon

1 large banana

1 tablespoon sesame seeds

2 tablespoons Greek yogurt

200 ml/7 fl oz whole or
 semi-skimmed milk

1 Put the cranberries and lemon juice in a food processor or blender and process until the berries are in small pieces.

2 Add the banana and sesame seeds and process to a purée, scraping the mixture down from the sides of the bowl at intervals if necessary.

3 Add the yogurt and milk, processing until smooth and frothy, then pour into a glass.

Nutritional information per serving:
Energy: 420 kcals/1765 kJ **Protein:** 16 g
Carbohydrate: 45 g **Fat:** 21 g **Fibre:** 10 g
Calcium: 478 mg **Iron:** 2.5 mg

Mango, orange & soya milkshake

**Makes 1 large
or 2 small glasses
Preparation:** 3 minutes

1 small ripe mango

juice of 1 orange

150 ml/¼ pint soya milk

1–2 teaspoons honey

1 Halve the mango and discard the stone. Scoop the flesh into a food processor or blender.

2 Add the orange juice, soya milk and 1 teaspoon of the honey. Process until smooth, scraping the mixture down from the sides of the bowl if necessary.

3 Taste for sweetness and, if it is needed, add a little more honey, then pour the milkshake into a glass.

Nutritional information per serving:
Energy: 200 kcals/853 kJ **Protein:** 6 g
Carbohydrate: 40 g **Fat:** 3 g **Fibre:** 5 g
Calcium: 50 mg **Iron:** 2 mg

Spicy fruit & seed bread

Makes 1 x 550 g/1 lb loaf
Preparation: 10 minutes
Cooking: 20–25 minutes

150 g/5 oz chickpea flour

150 g/5 oz gluten-free flour

2 teaspoons easy-blend dried yeast

1 teaspoon salt

1 teaspoon caster sugar

1 tablespoon black onion seeds

1 tablespoon cumin seeds

2 teaspoons ground coriander

¼ teaspoon dried chilli flakes

50 g/2 oz dried mango or pear, chopped

2 tablespoons refined ground-nut oil

200 ml/7 fl oz hand-hot water

1 Put the flours, yeast, salt, sugar, spices and dried fruit in a bowl and mix together.

2 Add the oil and water and mix to a stiff paste.

3 Turn into a greased 500 g/1 lb loaf tin, cover loosely with oiled cling film and leave in a warm place for about 45 minutes until the mixture rises slightly above the top of the tin. Remove the clingfilm.

4 Bake in a preheated oven, 200°C (400°F), Gas Mark 6, for 20–25 minutes until firm to the touch. Loosen the edges of the loaf with a knife and turn out on to a wire rack to cool.

TIP

With its lovely crumbly texture and intense flavours, this tasty bread makes a perfect lunch served with a simple tomato, onion and soft cheese salad.

Nutritional information per slice:
Energy: 172 kcals/727 kJ **Protein:** 6 g
Carbohydrate: 30 g **Fat:** 5 g **Fibre:** 4 g
Calcium: 55 mg **Iron:** 3 mg

Toasted open sandwiches

2 garlic cloves, crushed

3 tablespoons olive oil

4 slices gluten-free bread

200 g/7 oz roasted peppers

100 g/3½ oz firm goats' cheese,
   thinly sliced

black olives

1 tablespoon balsamic vinegar

salt and pepper

1 Mix the garlic with 2 tablespoons of the olive oil and a little seasoning. Put the bread on a baking sheet and toast it on one side. Turn the slices over, brush with the garlic oil and toast until golden.

2 Arrange the roasted peppers over the bread and top with the goats' cheese slices. Return to the grill and cook for about 1 minute to heat through.

3 Transfer the sandwiches to serving plates. Scatter the portions with several olives and drizzle with the remaining olive oil and balsamic vinegar.

VARIATION:

You can vary the toppings to suit your taste. Try a layer of ready-made pesto topped with halved cherry tomatoes and canned haricot beans, drained and rinsed. Drizzle with olive oil and balsamic vinegar.

Nutritional information per serving:
Energy: 570 kcals/2117 kJ **Protein:** 9 g
Carbohydrate: 35 g **Fat:** 37 g **Fibre:** 4 g
Calcium: 149 mg **Iron:** 1 mg

Chickpea flatbreads

Serves 4
Preparation: 20 minutes
Cooking: about 20 minutes

FLATBREADS:

150 g/5 oz chickpea flour

50 g/2 oz gluten-free flour

¼ teaspoon salt

2 tablespoons olive oil

75–100 ml/3–3½ fl oz milk

FILLING:

1 large aubergine, thinly sliced

2 courgettes, thinly sliced

2 tablespoons olive oil

2 tablespoons finely chopped oregano or rosemary

6 tablespoons sun-dried tomato paste

4 large tomatoes, thinly sliced

salt and pepper

1 To make the flatbreads, put the flours, salt and oil in a bowl. Add 75 ml/3 fl oz of the milk and mix with a round-bladed knife to a firm dough, adding a little more milk if the mixture is too dry. Knead lightly until smooth, then set aside.

2 Arrange the aubergine and courgette slices on a large foil-lined baking sheet. Season lightly and brush with a little oil. Sprinkle the herbs on top and grill for 6–8 minutes until golden. Turn the slices over, brush with the remaining oil, and grill the other side until golden.

3 Divide the chickpea dough into 4 pieces. Roll 1 piece out very thinly on a well-floured surface to a 23 cm/9 inch round, turning the dough frequently so it does not stick to the surface. Shape the remaining pieces in the same way.

4 Brush a large frying pan with a little oil and fry the flatbreads individually for about 1 minute each side.

5 Spread with the tomato paste and arrange the aubergine, courgette and tomato slices on top. Season and roll up to serve.

Nutritional information per serving:
Energy: 430 kcals/1796 kJ **Protein:** 12 g
Carbohydrate: 42 g **Fat:** 25 g **Fibre:** 10 g
Calcium: 124 mg **Iron:** 5 mg

Baked sweet potatoes with tomato salsa

Serves 2
Preparation: 5 minutes
Cooking: 45 minutes

2 large sweet potatoes, each
　about 275 g/9 oz

1 tablespoon olive oil

2 large tomatoes

½ small red onion, finely
　chopped

1 celery stick, finely chopped

small handful fresh coriander,
　chopped

2 tablespoons lime juice

2 teaspoons caster sugar

50 g/2 oz Emmental or
　Cheddar cheese, grated

salt

1 Scrub the potatoes and put them in a small roasting tin. Prick with a fork and drizzle with the oil and a little salt. Bake in a preheated oven, 200°C (400°F), Gas Mark 6, for 45 minutes until tender.

2 Meanwhile, finely chop the tomatoes and mix in a bowl with the onion, celery, coriander, lime juice and sugar.

3 Halve the potatoes and fluff up the flesh with a fork. Sprinkle with the cheese and serve topped with the salsa.

TIP

If you do not have the time to bake the potatoes, they can be microwaved like ordinary ones, although this way you will lose the wonderful crispy baked flavour. Prick them with a fork and cook on the highest setting for 15–20 minutes, or according to the manufacturer's instructions.

Nutritional information per serving:
Energy: 434 kcals/1835 kJ **Protein:** 12 g
Carbohydrate: 69 g **Fat:** 14 g **Fibre:** 9 g
Calcium: 333 mg **Iron:** 3 mg

Potato rosti

Serves 4
Preparation: 10 minutes
Cooking: 10 minutes

1 kg/2 lb small baking
   potatoes, unpeeled
1 small onion, thinly sliced
15 g/½ oz butter
2 tablespoons olive oil
salt and pepper

1 Leave the potatoes whole and cook in boiling, salted water for 10 minutes until softened but not completely tender. Drain and leave to cool.

2 Peel the skins from the potatoes and coarsely grate the flesh into a bowl. Stir in the onion and a little seasoning.

3 Heat the butter with the oil in a medium-sized, heavy-based, preferably nonstick frying pan. Tip the potato mixture into the pan and spread it in an even layer. Cook gently for about 10 minutes or until it is turning golden around the edges.

4 Shake the pan to loosen the potatoes, then, with a plate over the top, invert the pan so the potato cake comes out. Slide it back into the pan to cook the other side and fry for a further 10 minutes until it is done on the underside. Serve in wedges.

TIP

These crisp and golden rostis make an excellent base for tangy dressed bean or fish salads, or simply ham and eggs.

Nutritional information per serving:
Energy: 270 kcals/1134 kJ **Protein:** 5 g
Carbohydrate: 44 g **Fat:** 9 g **Fibre:** 9 g
Calcium: 17 mg **Iron:** 1 mg

Mascarpone, feta & herb pété

Serves 6
Preparation: 10 minutes

250 g/8 oz mascarpone cheese

6–8 tablespoons milk

200 g/7 oz feta cheese, cut into
small dice

½ celery stick, finely diced

50 g/2 oz pitted black olives,
roughly chopped

2 spring onions, finely chopped

2 garlic cloves, crushed

1 tablespoon fresh chopped
mint

1 tablespoon fresh chopped flat
leaf parsley

salt and pepper

1 Put the mascarpone into a bowl and beat lightly to soften. Stir in sufficient milk to give the consistency of thick yogurt.

2 Add the feta cheese to the bowl with the celery, olives, spring onions, garlic, herbs and seasoning, and gently fold the ingredients together until evenly combined.

3 Turn into a serving bowl, cover and chill until ready to serve.

Nutritional information per serving:
Energy: 270 kcals/1119 kJ **Protein:** 9 g
Carbohydrate: 3 g **Fat:** 25 g **Fibre:** 0 g
Calcium: 156 mg **Iron:** <1 mg

Chilli rice noodles

Serves 2
Preparation: 5 minutes
Cooking: 3 minutes

4 teaspoons seasoned rice
   vinegar

1 tablespoon caster sugar

1 teaspoon Thai fish sauce

1 tablespoon soy sauce

100 g/3½ oz dried rice ribbon
   noodles

1 tablespoon vegetable oil or
   refined groundnut oil

1 small red chilli, deseeded and
   finely shredded

1 small red pepper, deseeded
   and finely shredded

50 g/2 oz mangetout, sliced
   thinly lengthways

1 Mix together the vinegar, sugar, fish sauce and soy sauce. Put the noodles in a bowl and cover them with boiling water. Leave for 3–4 minutes until soft.

2 While the noodles are soaking, heat the oil in a frying pan and fry the chilli, red pepper and mangetout for 3 minutes until softened.

3 Drain the noodles and add to the pan with the sauce mixture. Toss together and serve immediately.

VARIATION:

Try spring onions, sugarsnap peas, mushrooms or French beans instead of peppers and mangetout.

TIP

Keep an eye on the noodles during soaking as they quickly become too soft. You must use them as soon as they are drained – they will stick together if left in the colander.

Nutritional information per serving:
Energy: 283 kcals/1180 kJ **Protein:** 4 g
Carbohydrate: 52 g **Fat:** 6 g **Fibre:** 2 g
Calcium: 29 mg **Iron:** 2 mg

Spiced & salted nuts

Makes 400 g/13 oz
Preparation: 3 minutes
Cooking: 3–4 minutes

15 g/½ oz butter

1 tablespoon light olive oil

400 g/13 oz whole mixed nuts
   (e.g. almonds, hazelnuts,
   walnuts, brazil nuts)

1 tablespoon ground paprika

½ teaspoon cayenne pepper

2 teaspoons cumin seeds,
   lightly crushed

sea salt flakes, for sprinkling

1 Melt the butter with the oil in a frying pan. Add the nuts and spices.

2 Gently fry the mixture, stirring continuously until the nuts are lightly coloured.

3 Remove from the heat and cool slightly. Strain with a slotted spoon into a bowl and season with salt. Store in an airtight container for up to one week.

TIP

For a milder flavour, reduce the quantity of cayenne pepper to ¼ teaspoon.

Nutritional information per serving:
Energy: 286 kcals/1180 kJ **Protein:** 7 g
Carbohydrate: 2 g **Fat:** 28 g **Fibre:** 4 g
Calcium: 67 mg **Iron:** 1.5 mg

Hummus

Serves 6
Preparation: 15 minutes,
plus overnight soaking
Cooking: about 1 hour

150 g/5 oz dried chickpeas

juice of 2 lemons

3 garlic cloves, roughly
   chopped

3 tablespoons olive oil

150 ml/¼ pint tahini paste

salt and pepper

extra olive oil, to drizzle
   (optional)

1 Put the chickpeas in a bowl, cover with plenty of water and leave to soak overnight. Drain and put in a saucepan with plenty of fresh water. Bring to the boil and boil rapidly for 10 minutes. Reduce the heat and simmer gently for 45–60 minutes until the chickpeas are completely tender. Drain well.

2 Tip the chickpeas into a food processor and process to a paste. Add the lemon juice, garlic, olive oil, tahini paste and seasoning, and blend until very smooth, scraping the mixture down from the sides of the bowl when necessary. The longer it is blended, the creamier the hummus will become.

3 Transfer to a serving bowl, cover and chill until ready to serve. Serve drizzled with extra olive oil if liked.

TIP

Homemade hummus is a delicious and versatile treat to have in the fridge. It can be used as a sandwich filler, as a topping for jacket potatoes or as a simple snack with vegetable sticks.

Nutritional information per serving:
Energy: 284 kcals/1180 kJ **Protein:** 10 g
Carbohydrate: 13 g **Fat:** 22 g **Fibre:** 3 g
Calcium: 212 mg **Iron:** 4 mg

Potato & onion tortilla

Serves 6
Preparation: 10 minutes
Cooking: 30 minutes

750 g/1½ lb baking potatoes

4 tablespoons olive oil

2 large onions, thinly sliced

6 eggs, beaten

salt and pepper

VARIATION:

Thinly sliced chorizo sausage, grated Parmesan cheese, garlic, fresh herbs and chopped peppers all make delicious additions to a tortilla. Mix them in with the onions.

1 Slice the potatoes very thinly and toss them in a bowl with a little seasoning. Heat the oil in a medium-sized, heavy-based frying pan. Add the potatoes and fry them very gently for 10 minutes, turning them frequently until they are softened but not browned.

2 Add the onions and fry them gently for a further 5 minutes without browning. Spread the potatoes and onions in an even layer in the pan and turn the heat down as low as possible.

3 Pour over the eggs, cover and cook very gently for about 15 minutes until the eggs have set. (If the centre of the omelette is too wet, put the pan under a moderate grill to finish cooking.) Tip the tortilla on to a plate and serve warm or cold.

TIP

Serve for a family lunch or supper with salad, chilling any leftovers for lunch boxes or snacks the following day.

Nutritional information per serving:
Energy: 296 kcals/1237 kJ **Protein:** 13 g
Carbohydrate: 28 g **Fat:** 16 g **Fibre:** 3 g
Calcium: 68 mg **Iron:** 2 mg

Potato pizza margherita

Serves 3–4
Preparation: 20 minutes
Cooking: 45 minutes

1 kg/2 lb baking potatoes

3 tablespoons olive oil

1 egg, beaten

50 g/2 oz Parmesan or Cheddar
cheese, freshly grated

4 tablespoons sun-dried tomato
paste or ketchup

500 g/1 lb small tomatoes,
thinly sliced

125 g/4 oz mozzarella cheese,
thinly sliced

1 tablespoons fresh chopped
thyme (optional)

salt

1 Cut the potatoes into small chunks and cook in boiling, lightly salted water for about 15 minutes until tender. Drain thoroughly, return to the pan and leave to cool for 10 minutes. Oil a large baking sheet.

2 Add 2 tablespoons of the oil, the egg and half the grated cheese to the potato, and mix well. Turn out on to the prepared baking sheet and spread to a 25 cm/10 inch round. Bake in a preheated oven, 200°C (400°F), Gas Mark 6, for 15 minutes.

3 Remove from the oven and spread with the tomato paste or ketchup. Arrange the tomato and mozzarella slices on top. Scatter with the remaining grated cheese, thyme if using and a little salt. Drizzle with the remaining oil.

4 Return to the oven for a further 15 minutes until the potato is crisp around the edges and the cheese is melting.

TIP

Mini potato pizzas are a great idea for children's parties. Simply divide the potato mixture into six circles on a baking sheet.

Nutritional information per serving:
Energy: 633 kcals/2655 kJ **Protein:** 28 g
Carbohydrate: 70 g **Fat:** 28 g **Fibre:** 8 g
Calcium: 93 mg **Iron:** 1 mg

Homemade veggie sausages & beans

Serves 6
Preparation: 30 minutes, plus overnight soaking
Cooking: about 2 hours

250 g/8 oz dried haricot beans

2 teaspoons cornflour

300 ml/½ pint vegetable stock

2 tablespoons olive oil

2 onions, chopped

400 g/13 oz can chopped
   tomatoes

1 tablespoon grainy mustard

2 tablespoons black treacle

2 tablespoons tomato ketchup

SAUSAGES:

300 g/10 oz potatoes

2 small carrots, finely grated

1 large onion, finely chopped

100 g/3½ oz Cheddar cheese,
   grated

100 g/3½ oz gluten-free
   breadcrumbs

1 egg

salt and pepper

a little oil for frying

1 Soak the beans overnight in plenty of cold water. Drain, put in a pan and cover with fresh water. Boil rapidly for 10 minutes, then reduce the heat and simmer gently for 30 minutes until tender. Drain and turn into a casserole dish.

2 Blend the cornflour with 4 tablespoons of water until smooth. Add the stock and pour over the beans. Then add the oil, onions, tomatoes, mustard, treacle and ketchup, stirring everything together to mix well. Cook in a preheated oven, 170°C (325°F), Gas Mark 3, for 1½–2 hours until the beans are tender and the sauce has thickened.

3 Meanwhile, make the sausages. Dice the potato and cook in boiling water for 5 minutes until soft. Drain thoroughly, return to the pan and mash until smooth.

4 Turn the mash into a bowl and add the remaining ingredients (apart from the oil). Season lightly and mix thoroughly. Divide into 12 portions and shape each into a thick sausage.

5 Heat the oil in a frying pan and cook the sausages for about 10 minutes turning frequently until golden. Serve with beans.

Nutritional information per serving:
Energy: 409 kcals/1722 kJ **Protein:** 18 g
Carbohydrate: 55 g **Fat:** 14 g **Fibre:** 13 g
Calcium: 290 mg **Iron:** 5 mg

Little cottage pies

Serves 8–10
Preparation: 25 minutes
Cooking: 1 hour 10 minutes

2 onions, very roughly chopped

400 g/13 oz carrots, cut into
   large pieces

4 celery sticks, cut into chunks

50 g/2 oz butter

2 tablespoons olive oil

550 g/1 lb 2 oz lean lamb
   mince

500 ml/17 fl oz chicken or
   lamb stock

4 tablespoons tomato ketchup

2 tablespoons chopped oregano
   or rosemary

2 kg/4 lb large potatoes

150 ml/¼ pint whole milk

400 g/13 oz can baked beans

salt and pepper

1 Put the onions, carrots and celery in a food processor and process until very finely chopped. Heat half the butter with the oil in a large saucepan, add the vegetables and fry, stirring for 5 minutes until they begin to colour. Add the meat and fry, breaking it up with a wooden spoon for a further 5 minutes.

2 Add the stock, ketchup, herb and a little seasoning, and bring to the boil. Reduce the heat, cover with a lid and simmer gently for 20 minutes, stirring occasionally.

3 Meanwhile, cut the potatoes into chunks and cook in lightly salted, boiling water for 15–20 minutes until tender. Drain and return to the saucepan. Mash well and stir in the remaining butter and the milk.

4 Stir the baked beans into the meat mixture. Turn into a large, shallow ovenproof dish or individual foil or pie dishes. Spoon the potatoes over the filling, spreading it right to the edges.

5 Bake in a preheated oven, 200°C (400°F), Gas Mark 6, for about 40 minutes until the potato is pale golden.

Nutritional information per serving:
Energy: 470 kcals/1970 kJ **Protein:** 24 g
Carbohydrate: 62 g **Fat:** 16 g **Fibre:** 10 g
Calcium: 100 mg **Iron:** 3 mg

Corn & bacon muffins

Makes 12
Preparation: 10 minutes
Cooking: 20 minutes

6 streaky bacon rashers

1 small red onion, finely
chopped

200 g/7 oz frozen sweetcorn

175 g/6 oz fine cornmeal

125 g/4 oz gluten-free plain
flour

2 teaspoons Gluten-free baking
powder (see page 42)

50 g/2 oz Cheddar cheese,
grated

200 ml/7 fl oz semi-skimmed
milk

2 eggs

3 tablespoons vegetable oil

1 Lightly oil a 12-section muffin tin. Cut off any rind and excess fat, then finely chop the bacon and dry-fry it in a pan with the onion over a moderate heat for 3–4 minutes until the bacon is turning crisp. Cook the sweetcorn in boiling water for 2 minutes to soften.

2 Put the cornmeal, flour and baking powder in a bowl and mix together. Add the sweetcorn, cheese, bacon and onions, and stir in.

3 Whisk the milk with the eggs and oil and add to the bowl. Stir gently until combined, then divide among the tin sections.

4 Bake in a preheated oven, 220°C (425°F), Gas Mark 7, for 15–20 minutes until golden and just firm. Loosen the edges of the muffins with a knife and transfer to a wire rack to cool.

VARIATION:

For a vegetarian version, replace the bacon with an extra 25 g/1 oz cheese and add salt and pepper.

Nutritional information per serving:
Energy: 228 kcals/954 kJ **Protein:** 7 g
Carbohydrate: 26 g **Fat:** 11 g **Fibre:** 1 g
Calcium: 68 mg **Iron:** 1 mg

Sticky chicken drumsticks

Makes 16 drumsticks
Preparation: 5 minutes
Cooking: 50 minutes

16 chicken drumsticks

4 tablespoons honey

finely grated rind and juice of 1 lemon

finely grated rind and juice of 1 orange

3 tablespoons Worcestershire sauce

4 tablespoons tomato ketchup

1 Make several diagonal cuts through the fleshy part of each chicken drumstick and arrange in a single layer in a roasting tin or shallow ovenproof dish.

2 Mix together the remaining ingredients and spoon over the chicken. Cover and chill until ready to cook.

3 Cook in a preheated oven, 180°C (350°F), Gas Mark 4, for about 50 minutes, turning the chicken and basting frequently until the chicken is cooked through and thickly coated with the sticky glaze. Serve hot or chill thoroughly for serving cold.

TIP

For the perfect accompaniment make some homemade oven chips. Scrub 1 kg/2 lb baking potatoes, cut them into small wedges and put them in one layer in a roasting tin. Drizzle with vegetable oil and season with salt, turning the potatoes so they are well covered in oil. Bake with the chicken until they are pale golden.

Nutritional information per serving:
Energy: 133 kcals/558 kJ **Protein:** 15 g
Carbohydrate: 7 g **Fat:** 5 g **Fibre:** 0 g
Calcium: 16 mg **Iron:** 1 mg

Chocolate fudge crisps

Makes 24
Preparation: 15 minutes
Cooking: 2 minutes

75 g/3 oz fudge

75 g/3 oz milk chocolate

75 g/3 oz unsalted butter

3 tablespoons golden syrup

25 g/1 oz cocoa powder

150 g/5 oz puffed rice cereal

1 Place 24 paper cases on a large tray or baking sheet. Chop the fudge and chocolate into small dice and set aside.

2 Put the butter and syrup in a large saucepan and heat gently, stirring until the butter melts. Stir in the cocoa powder and remove from the heat. Stir in the cereal until well coated.

3 Add the chopped chocolate and fudge to the mixture. Spoon into the cases, packing the mixture down gently, and leave to set. Store in an airtight container for up to 3 days.

VARIATION:

Substitute 125 g/4 oz raisins or sultanas for the fudge if preferred.

Nutritional information per crisp:
Energy: 89 kcals/373 kJ **Protein:** 1 g
Carbohydrate: 13 g **Fat:** 4 g **Fibre:** 0 g
Calcium: 14 mg **Iron:** <1 mg

Flower fairy cakes

Makes 18
Preparation: 25 minutes, plus cooling
Cooking: 25 minutes

50 g/2 oz **ground almonds**

75 g/3 oz **gluten-free plain flour**

1 teaspoon **Gluten-free baking powder** (see page 42)

125 g/4 oz **unsalted butter, softened**

125 g/4 oz **golden caster sugar**

2 **eggs**

finely grated rind of 1 lemon, plus 3 tablespoons juice

225 g/7½ oz **icing sugar**

orange and yellow food colouring

VARIATION:

If you'd prefer to leave out the nuts, use an additional 50 g/2 oz gluten-free flour instead.

1 Line tartlet trays with 18 paper cases.

2 Put the almonds, flour, baking powder, butter, sugar, eggs and lemon rind in a large bowl. Beat with a hand-held electric whisk for about 2 minutes until smooth and creamy.

3 Using teaspoons, divide the mixture among the paper cases. Bake in a preheated oven at 180°C (350°F), Gas Mark 4, for 20–25 minutes until golden and just firm to touch. Transfer to a wire rack to cool.

4 To decorate, put the lemon juice in a bowl and whisk in the icing sugar to make a smooth paste. Transfer half to another bowl and colour one half orange, the other yellow.

5 Put a dessertspoonful of each colour icing in a polythene bag and squeeze into a corner. Cut off the merest tip so the icing can be piped from the corner. Spoon the remaining icing over the cakes, spreading to the corners with a palette knife.

6 Using the icing in the bags, pipe simple flower shapes over the cakes so the colours contrast. Alternatively pipe the children's initials or a message on to the cakes.

Nutritional information per cake:
Energy: 169 kcals/710 kJ **Protein:** 2 g
Carbohydrate: 24 g **Fat:** 8 g **Fibre:** 1 g
Calcium: 18 mg **Iron:** 0 mg

Rainbow lollies

Makes 12
Preparation: 20 minutes

1 large ripe mango

4 kiwi fruit

300 g/10 oz strawberries

375 g/12 oz blackberries or
   blueberries

VARIATION:

Almost any fruit can be used for lollies, as long as it is really ripe and therefore soft and sweet. If you do not have the time to make layered lollies, simply use a selection of different flavours. Stir in a little honey or sugar to sweeten the fruits, if desired.

1 Halve the mango and discard the stone. Scoop the flesh into a food processor or blender and process to a smooth purée, scraping the fruit down from the sides of the bowl if necessary.

2 Pour into a small jug (if the mixture is too thick to pour, thin with a little orange juice or water). Quarter-fill 12 lolly moulds with the mango juice and put in the freezer for about 30 minutes to set.

3 Meanwhile, prepare the other fruit. Peel the kiwi fruit, purée and put in a clean jug. Hull and blend the strawberries, then press through a sieve over a bowl to remove the seeds. Blend the blackberries or blueberries and press through a sieve into a separate bowl.

4 Pour a layer of kiwi juice over the mango and return to the freezer. Add the strawberry purée, pushing in the lolly sticks once it is beginning to freeze. Finish with the blackberry or blueberry layer and return to the freezer, where the lollies can be kept for up to 6 months.

5 To serve, run the moulds quickly under very hot water to loosen the lollies, then gently pull them out.

Nutritional information per lolly:
Energy: 30 kcals/133 kJ **Protein:** 1 g
Carbohydrate: 7 g **Fat:** 0 g **Fibre:** 3 g
Calcium: 23 mg **Iron:** 0.5 mg

Chocolate biscuit log

Makes about 20 slices
Preparation: 10 minutes
Cooking: 2 minutes

1 tablespoon groundnut oil

50 g/2 oz popping corn

100 g/3½ oz milk chocolate

100 g/3½ oz plain chocolate

25 g/1 oz butter

75 g/3 oz nuts and raisins

50 g/2 oz white chocolate
buttons

VARIATION:

For a more sophisticated adult version, you could use 200 g/7 oz plain chocolate instead of the mix of milk and plain, and milk chocolate rather than white chocolate buttons.

1 To make the popcorn, heat the oil in a heavy-based saucepan with a tight-fitting lid. Add the corn and heat very gently until the corn starts to pop, shaking the pan frequently.

2 Once the popping subsides, remove the pan from the heat and wait for a minute or so until the popping stops completely. Weigh 200 g/7 oz of the corn. Once it is cool enough to handle, crush it with your hands into smaller pieces.

3 Melt the chocolate with the butter in a large bowl. Stir in the crushed corn and nuts and raisins until evenly combined. Gently stir in the chocolate buttons.

4 Lay a sheet of baking parchment on your surface and spoon the chocolate mixture across the centre. Bring the paper up around the chocolate mixture, shaping and packing it into a roll about 30 cm/12 inches long. Chill for at least 2 hours until firm.

5 To serve, unwrap the roll and cut into chunky slices with a sharp knife.

Nutritional information per serving:
Energy: 119 kcals/495 kJ **Protein:** 2 g
Carbohydrate: 11 g **Fat:** 8 g **Fibre:** 0 g
Calcium: 22 mg **Iron:** <1 mg

Chocolate lover's birthday cake

Serves 12–14
Preparation: 30 minutes, plus cooling
Cooking: 25 minutes

175 g/6 oz unsalted butter, softened

175 g/6 oz golden caster sugar

3 eggs

2 teaspoons vanilla extract

25 g/1 oz cocoa powder

175 g/6 oz gluten-free flour

1 teaspoon Gluten-free baking powder (see page 42)

100 g/3½ oz milk chocolate, chopped

ICING:

200 g/7 oz plain chocolate

4 tablespoons milk

40 g/1½ oz unsalted butter

175 g/6 oz golden icing sugar

selection of small chocolates or chocolate bars, cut into chunks, to decorate

cocoa powder and icing sugar, to dust

1 Grease and line the bases of a couple of 20 cm/8 inch round sandwich tins.

2 Put the butter, sugar, eggs, vanilla, cocoa powder, flour and baking powder in a mixing bowl and beat for about 2 minutes until smooth and creamy.

3 Divide between the prepared tins, scatter with the chopped milk chocolate and level the surfaces. Bake in a preheated oven, 180°C (350°F), Gas Mark 4, for 25 minutes or until firm to the touch. Transfer to a wire rack to cool.

4 To finish the cake, break the plain chocolate into pieces and put in a saucepan with the milk and butter. Heat over the lowest setting until the chocolate has melted, stirring frequently. Beat in the icing sugar until smooth.

5 Use a little of the icing to sandwich the cakes together and transfer to a serving plate. Spread the remaining icing over the top and sides of the cakes, swirling with a palette knife.

6 Position the birthday candles, if you are using them, and pile plenty of chocolate around the top edges of the cake to decorate, pressing the pieces gently into the icing to secure them. Lightly dust with cocoa power and icing sugar.

Nutritional information per serving:
Energy: 460 kcals/1929 kJ **Protein:** 5 g
Carbohydrate: 59 g **Fat:** 24 g **Fibre:** <1 g
Calcium: 48 mg **Iron:** 1 mg

Chicken & ham soup

Serves 8
Preparation: 20 minutes
Cooking: 1 hour, 20 minutes

375 g/12 oz piece lean
  gammon

3 tablespoons olive oil

4 large chicken thighs, skinned

3 medium onions, chopped

2 celery sticks, sliced

2 bay leaves

600 ml/1 pint chicken stock

375 g/12 oz potatoes, cut into
  small dice

150 g/5 oz frozen sweetcorn

DUMPLINGS:

125 g/4 oz fine cornmeal

100 g/3½ oz gluten-free flour

2 teaspoons Gluten-free baking
  powder (see page 42)

1 tablespoon chopped fresh
  thyme

40 g/1½ oz chilled butter

salt and pepper

1 Chop the gammon into 1 cm/½ inch chunks. Heat the oil in a large, heavy-based saucepan. Add the chicken, onions and celery, and fry gently for 10 minutes, stirring until golden.

2 Add the gammon, bay leaves, stock and 600 ml/1 pint water, and bring to the boil. Reduce the heat, cover and simmer gently for 40 minutes until the chicken and ham are tender.

3 Pick out the chicken with a slotted spoon and, when cool enough to handle, shred the flesh from the bones. Return to the pan with the potatoes and sweetcorn. Simmer, covered, for 20 minutes, until the potatoes are tender.

4 To make the dumplings, mix together the cornmeal, flour, baking powder, thyme and seasoning until evenly combined. Grate the butter into the mixture and add 250 ml/8 fl oz water. Mix to a thick paste, adding a little more water if necessary.

5 Using 2 dessertspoons, roughly pat the paste into 8 rounds and spoon into the soup. Cover and simmer gently for about 10 minutes until the dumplings are light and puffy. Serve hot.

Nutritional information per serving:
Energy: 334 kcals/1396 kJ **Protein:** 17 g
Carbohydrate: 36 g **Fat:** 14 g **Fibre:** 2 g
Calcium: 45 mg **Iron:** 2 mg

Parsnip & fresh ginger soup

25 g/1 oz butter

750 g/1½ lb parsnips, sliced

2 large onions, roughly
   chopped

1.2 litres/2 pints chicken or
   vegetable stock

25 g/1 oz fresh root ginger,
   grated

200 ml/7 fl oz crème fraîche

salt and pepper (optional)

1 Melt the butter in a large saucepan. Add the parsnips and onions, and fry very gently for 10 minutes until softened but not browned.

2 Add the stock and bring to the boil. Reduce the heat, cover and simmer gently for 20 minutes until the parsnips are tender. Stir in the ginger. Blend the mixture in a food processor or using a hand-held electric wand until smooth.

3 Add half the crème fraîche and heat through, adding a little seasoning if liked. Ladle into soup bowls and swirl in the remaining crème fraîche to serve.

Nutritional information per serving:
Energy: 268 kcals/1115 kJ **Protein:** 4 g
Carbohydrate: 23 g **Fat:** 18 g **Fibre:** 7 g
Calcium: 73 mg **Iron:** 1 mg

Lentil & rosemary soup

Serves 5–6
Preparation: 10 minutes
Cooking: 45 minutes

250 g/8 oz green lentils

3 tablespoons olive oil

2 onions, chopped

3 garlic cloves, chopped

¼ teaspoon ground turmeric

1 tablespoon freshly chopped
  rosemary

2 bay leaves

900 ml/1½ pints vegetable
  stock

small handful chopped flat leaf
  parsley

salt and pepper

Greek yogurt, to serve
  (optional)

1 Put the lentils in a saucepan, cover with water and bring to the boil. Boil rapidly for 10 minutes, then drain.

2 Heat the oil in a large saucepan and fry the onions for 5 minutes until lightly browned. Add the garlic, turmeric, rosemary, bay leaves, lentils and stock and bring to the boil.

3 Reduce the heat, cover and simmer gently for about 30 minutes until the lentils are completely soft. Use a hand-held electric wand to lightly pulp the soup, adding a little more stock if it becomes too thick. (Alternatively use a potato masher to pulp the mixture.)

4 Season to taste, stir in the parsley and serve in bowl, with spoonfuls of yogurt, if liked.

TIP

As well as making an appetizing starter, this nutritious soup can double as a light meal when served in larger bowls with chunks of warm bread.

Nutritional information per serving:
Energy: 230 kcals/980 kJ **Protein:** 13 g
Carbohydrate: 30 g **Fat:** 8 g **Fibre:** 1 g
Calcium: 57 mg **Iron:** 6 mg

Chilled gazpacho

Serves 6
Preparation: 20 minutes

875 g/1¾ lb tomatoes, skinned
and roughly chopped

½ cucumber, roughly chopped

2 red peppers, deseeded and
roughly chopped

1 stick celery, chopped

2 garlic cloves, chopped

½ red chilli, deseeded and
sliced

small handful fresh coriander
or flat leaf parsley

2 tablespoons white wine
vinegar

2 tablespoons sun-dried tomato
paste

4 tablespoons olive oil

ice cubes

salt

extra parsley or coriander, to
garnish

1 Mix together the vegetables, garlic, chilli and coriander in a
large bowl.

2 Add the vinegar, tomato paste, oil and a little salt. Process in
batches in a food processor or blender until smooth, scraping
the mixture down from the sides of the bowl if necessary.

3 Collect the blended mixtures in a clean bowl and check the
seasoning, adding a little more salt if needed. Chill for up to
24 hours before serving.

4 To serve, ladle into large bowls, scatter with ice cubes and
garnish with chopped parsley or coriander.

TIP

Traditionally, gazpacho is served
with little bowls of chopped
garnishes such as hard-boiled egg,
cucumber, pepper, parsley and
onion for sprinkling over the soup
for extra flavour.

Nutritional information per serving:
Energy: 135 kcals/560 kJ **Protein:** 2 g
Carbohydrate: 8 g **Fat:** 11 g **Fibre:** 3 g
Calcium: 20 mg **Iron:** 1 mg

Thai prawn & noodle soup

Serves 4
Preparation: 5 minutes
Cooking: 5 minutes

1 bunch spring onions

200 g/7 oz pak choy or green
cabbage

1.2 litres/2 pints rich chicken
stock

1 tablespoon light muscovado
sugar

2 tablespoons seasoned rice
vinegar

1 tablespoon soy sauce

2 tablespoons sesame oil

50 g/2 oz dried stir-fry rice
noodles

50 g/2 oz fresh root ginger,
finely chopped

200 g/7 oz peeled prawns

1 Slice the spring onions diagonally, then shred the pak choy or cabbage.

2 Put the stock, sugar, vinegar and soy sauce in a large saucepan and bring to the boil.

3 Gently heat the oil in a frying pan. Add the spring onions and greens and cook very gently for 3 minutes to soften.

4 Break the noodles into short lengths and add to the stock with the vegetables, ginger and prawns. Heat through gently for 2 minutes and serve immediately.

Nutritional information per serving:
Energy: 189 kcals/794 kJ **Protein:** 14 g
Carbohydrate: 18 g **Fat:** 7 g **Fibre:** 2 g
Calcium: 119 mg **Iron:** 2 mg

Millet 'tabbouleh'

Serves 4–6
Preparation: 10 minutes
Cooking: 10 minutes

250 g/8 oz millet

15 g/½ oz flat leaf parsley,
   finely chopped

15 g/½ oz mint, finely chopped

½ bunch spring onions, finely
   sliced

50 g/2 oz pine nuts, toasted

100 g/3½ oz red grapes, halved

2 tablespoons lemon juice

4 tablespoons extra virgin olive
   oil

salt and pepper

1 Cook the millet in plenty of boiling, lightly salted water for 10 minutes or until the grains are soft but not turning to a pulp. Strain through a sieve then pass under cold running water to cool. Drain thoroughly and tip into a salad bowl.

2 Stir in the remaining ingredients until well combined. Cover and chill to let the flavours mingle until ready to serve.

TIP

Here, millet replaces the couscous traditionally used in tabbouleh. It can be served with cold meats or cheese or used as a base for salad – try adding toasted seeds, chopped dried apricots or prunes, halved cherry tomatoes, sliced radishes or lightly cooked vegetables such as asparagus and sugarsnap peas.

Nutritional information per serving:
Energy: 429 kcals/1785 kJ **Protein:** 6 g
Carbohydrate: 53 g **Fat:** 21 g **Fibre:** 1 g
Calcium: 53 mg **Iron:** 2 mg

Walnut, pear & green leaf salad

Serves 4
Preparation: 10 minutes
Cooking: 3 minutes

75 g/3 oz freshly grated
   Parmesan cheese

6 tablespoons walnut oil

2 tablespoons lemon juice

1 tablespoon grainy mustard

2 teaspoons caster sugar

several fresh tarragon sprigs,
   roughly chopped

2 large, ripe pears

50 g/2 oz walnut pieces, lightly
   toasted

125 g/4 oz mixed leaf salad
   (e.g. watercress, rocket,
   spinach)

salt and pepper

1 Oil a foil-lined baking sheet and scatter the Parmesan cheese over it, spreading it to a thin layer about 25 cm/10 inches square. Cook under a preheated grill for 2–3 minutes until the cheese has melted and is pale golden. Leave until cool enough to handle, then peel the foil away, letting the cheese break into pieces to form 'croutes'.

2 Whisk together the oil, lemon juice, mustard, sugar, tarragon and seasoning. Halve and core the pears and cut into thin slices.

3 Toss the walnuts and pears with the salad leaves and dressing. Pile on to serving plates and scatter with the Parmesan croutes.

VARIATION:

Tarragon is lovely with sweet pears but other herbs, such as flat leaf parsley or fennel, also go well.

Nutritional information per serving:
Energy: 395 kcals/1640 kJ **Protein:** 11 g
Carbohydrate: 16 g **Fat:** 32 g **Fibre:** 2 g
Calcium: 300 mg **Iron:** 2 mg

Buckwheat blinis with smoked fish

Serves 6
Preparation: 20 minutes
Cooking: 10 minutes

BLINIS:

175 g/6 oz buckwheat flour

1 teaspoon Gluten-free baking
   powder (see page 42)

¼ teaspoon salt

2 eggs

250 ml/8 fl oz whole milk

oil for frying

TO SERVE:

2 tablespoons chopped fennel
   or tarragon

200 g/7 oz crème fraîche

200 g/7 oz smoked salmon or
   trout

salt and pepper

TO GARNISH:

lemon or lime wedges

fennel sprigs or chives

1 Mix together the buckwheat flour, baking powder and salt in a bowl and make a well in the centre.

2 Break the eggs into the well and add a little of the milk. Whisk the milk and eggs together, gradually incorporating the flour to make a smooth paste. Whisk in the remaining milk and pour into a jug.

3 Stir the herbs into the crème fraîche and season lightly.

4 Heat a little oil in a large frying pan over a low heat. Carefully pour some of the batter mixture into the pan so that it spreads to a small cake about 6 cm/2½ inches in diameter. Pour several more pancakes into the pan, keeping them spaced slightly apart. Cook for 30–45 seconds until golden on the underside, then turn over with a palette knife and cook for a further 1 minute. Drain on kitchen paper and keep warm while cooking the remainder.

5 Place the blinis, 3 per serving, on plates and top each with a little crème fraîche. Lay pieces of smoked fish over the crème fraîche. Garnish with lemon or lime wedges and sprigs of herbs.

Nutritional information per serving:
Energy: 363 kcals/1510 kJ **Protein:** 15 g
Carbohydrate: 28 g **Fat:** 22 g **Fibre:** 2 g
Calcium: 77 mg **Iron:** 1 mg

Fish cakes with fennel mayonnaise

Serves 4
Preparation: 20 minutes
Cooking: 20 minutes

500 g/1 lb cod or haddock
   fillets, skin and bones
   removed

4 tablespoons milk

750g/1½ lb baking potatoes

25 g/1 oz butter

2 tablespoons capers, rinsed
   and chopped

1 medium egg

75 g/3 oz polenta

sunflower or light olive oil for
   frying

6 tablespoons mayonnaise

3 tablespoons natural yogurt

3 tablespoons freshly chopped
   fennel

2 teaspoons hot horseradish
   sauce

salt and pepper

1 Cut the fish into chunky pieces and put in a frying pan with the milk and a little seasoning. Cover and cook gently for 5 minutes until just cooked through.

2 Meanwhile, cook the potatoes in boiling salted water for 15 minutes until tender. Drain, tip into a bowl and mash with a fork into chunky pieces.

3 Add the butter, capers, fish, 2 tablespoons of the cooking juices and seasoning. Mix together until the ingredients are combined but the fish and potatoes are still chunky. Shape the mixture into 8–10 balls and flatten into cakes.

4 Lightly beat the egg on a plate. Sprinkle the polenta on to another plate. Coat the fish cakes first in the egg and then in the polenta.

5 Heat 5 mm/¼ inch of oil in a large frying pan and fry the fish cakes, in batches if necessary, for about 2 minutes on each side until golden.

6 While they are cooking, mix together the mayonnaise, yogurt, fennel and horseradish, and transfer to a serving dish. Serve with the hot fish cakes.

Nutritional information per serving:
Energy: 667 kcals/2780 kJ **Protein:** 32 g
Carbohydrate: 50 g **Fat:** 39 g **Fibre:** 3 g
Calcium: 123 mg **Iron:** 2 mg

Baked trout with pine nuts

Serves 4
Preparation: 10 minutes
Cooking: 15–20 minutes

butter for greasing

4 trout fillets, each about
    125 g/4 oz, skinned

2 tablespoons olive oil

50 g/2 oz pine nuts

1 small onion, chopped

1 garlic clove, sliced

200 g/7 oz baby spinach

25 g/1 oz freshly grated
    Parmesan cheese

salt and pepper

1 Lightly butter a shallow ovenproof dish or roasting tin. Lay the trout fillets in the dish, season lightly and drizzle with 1 tablespoon of the oil. Bake in a preheated oven, 190°C (375°F), Gas Mark 5, for 5 minutes.

2 Heat the remaining oil in a frying pan and fry the pine nuts and onion for about 3 minutes until beginning to colour. Stir in the garlic and spinach, and mix together until the spinach has wilted.

3 Spoon the mixture over the trout and sprinkle with the cheese. Return to the oven for a further 6–8 minutes until the fish is cooked through.

TIP

Trout is quick to cook and makes a lighter alternative to salmon in this quickly assembled supper dish. Buy ready-prepared trout fillets to save you the trouble of filleting and boning the whole fish.

Nutritional information per serving:
Energy: 358 kcals/1490 kJ **Protein:** 35 g
Carbohydrate: 3 g **Fat:** 23 g **Fibre:** 2 g
Calcium: 210 mg **Iron:** 3 mg

Mediterranean lamb casserole

Serves 6
Preparation: 20 minutes
Cooking: about 1½ hours

1 kg/2 lb lean lamb, diced

1 kg/2 lb tomatoes, skinned

1 medium aubergine

2 red onions

6 tablespoons olive oil

3 red peppers, deseeded and
   cut into chunks

2 courgettes, thickly sliced

4 garlic cloves, sliced

3 tablespoons sun-dried tomato
   paste

6 rosemary sprigs

salt and pepper

1 Pat the lamb dry on kitchen paper and season lightly. Roughly chop the tomatoes. Cut the aubergine into small chunks. Cut the onions into thin wedges.

2 Heat 3 tablespoons of the oil in a large frying pan or sauté pan and fry the meat in batches until deep golden. Remove from the pan and drain. Add the onions to the pan and fry until golden, then remove from the pan and set aside.

3 Add the remaining oil to the pan with the aubergine, peppers and courgettes, and fry for 5–10 minutes until lightly browned.

4 Return the meat and onions to the pan with the garlic, tomatoes, tomato paste, rosemary and seasoning. Bring to the boil, reduce the heat and cover with a lid. Cook gently, stirring occasionally, for about 1 hour until the lamb is tender and the vegetables are pulpy. Serve hot with rice, polenta or new potatoes.

TIP

This dish freezes well. Pack into ovenproof or foil dishes and freeze for up to 3 months. Defrost overnight in the fridge.

Nutritional information per serving:
Energy: 488 kcals/2036 kJ **Protein:** 38 g
Carbohydrate: 16 g **Fat:** 30 g **Fibre:** 5 g
Calcium: 52 mg **Iron:** 5 mg

Loin of pork with lentils

175 g/6 oz Puy lentils

875 g/1¾ lb pork loin, skinned, boned and rolled

2 tablespoons olive oil

2 large onions, sliced

3 garlic cloves, sliced

1 tablespoon finely chopped fresh rosemary

300 ml/½ pint chicken or vegetable stock

250 g/8 oz baby carrots, scrubbed and left whole

salt and pepper

1 Put the lentils in a pan, cover with water and bring to the boil. Boil rapidly for 10 minutes, then drain and set aside.

2 Sprinkle the pork with salt and pepper. Heat the oil in a large heavy-based frying pan and brown the meat on all sides. Transfer to a casserole dish and add the lentils.

3 Add the onions to the pan and fry for 5 minutes. Add the garlic, rosemary and stock, and bring to the boil. Pour over the meat and lentils and cover with a lid. Cook in a preheated oven, 180°C (350°F), Gas Mark 4, for 1 hour.

4 Add the carrots and seasoning and return to the oven for a further 20–30 minutes until the pork and lentils are tender. Drain the meat, transfer to a serving platter and carve thin slices. Serve with the lentils and juices.

TIP

This flavoursome dish is good at any time of year – in winter served with heaps of roast potatoes and wintry vegetables, or in summer with buttery new potatoes.

Nutritional information per serving:
Energy: 527 kcals/2200 kJ **Protein:** 36 g
Carbohydrate: 28 g **Fat:** 31 g **Fibre:** 3 g
Calcium: 80 mg **Iron:** 5 mg

Spiced beef with spinach

Serves 4–5
Preparation: 15 minutes
Cooking: 1½ hours

12 cardamom pods

2 teaspoons cumin seeds

2 teaspoons coriander seeds

750 g/1½ lb lean braising beef,
    diced

3 tablespoons vegetable oil

2 onions, chopped

½ teaspoon ground turmeric

15 g/½ oz fresh root ginger,
    peeled and finely chopped

1 mild red chilli, deseeded and
    sliced

4 garlic cloves, thinly sliced

2 teaspoons caster sugar

400 g/13 oz can chopped
    tomatoes

200 ml/7 fl oz beef or chicken
    stock

300 g/10 oz baby spinach

salt and pepper

1 Crush the cardamom pods using a pestle and mortar to release the seeds. Discard the pods. Add the cumin and coriander and crush the seeds fairly finely.

2 Discard any excess fat from the beef and season lightly. Heat the oil in a large, heavy-based saucepan and fry the beef until it is browned. Add the onions, the crushed spices and turmeric and fry for 5 minutes, stirring.

3 Add the ginger, chilli, garlic, sugar, tomatoes and stock, and bring to the boil. Reduce the heat, cover with a lid and simmer very gently for about 1¼ hours until the beef is tender.

4 Pack the spinach into the pan and cover with the lid. Cook for about 5 minutes until the spinach has wilted. Stir the spinach into the sauce, season to taste and serve.

TIP

If you do not have a good selection of spices or simply want a short-cut version, use 2 teaspoons of medium curry paste instead of the separate spices.

Nutritional information per serving:
Energy: 390 kcals/1640 kJ **Protein:** 43 g
Carbohydrate: 14 g **Fat:** 18 g **Fibre:** 5 g
Calcium: 193 mg **Iron:** 7 mg

Summer roast chicken

Serves 4
Preparation: 15 minutes
Cooking: 1¼ hours

1.1 kg/2¼ lb chicken

1 small stalk lemon grass

100 g/3½ oz cream cheese

2 garlic cloves, crushed

2 tablespoons chopped chives

1 tablespoon chopped thyme

2 tablespoons chopped flat leaf
 parsley

1 small lemon, cut into wedges

1 lime, cut into wedges

salt and pepper

extra herbs, to garnish

VARIATION:

Almost any herb can be used in
this recipe: try tarragon,
rosemary, fennel or dill.

1 Wash the chicken and pat it dry with kitchen paper. Using
your fingers, loosen the skin away from the breast meat and
the tops of the thighs.

2 Trim and very finely chop the lemon grass. Beat the cream
cheese in a bowl with the lemon grass, garlic, herbs and a
little seasoning. Using a teaspoon, pack the stuffing under the
chicken skin, pushing it as far over the chicken thighs as you
can reach without tearing the skin. Push the skin back in
place, spreading the stuffing in an even layer.

3 Put the chicken in a roasting tin. Roast in a preheated oven,
190°C (375°F), Gas Mark 5, for 1¼ hours, adding the lemon
and lime wedges for the last 30 minutes of the cooking time.
To test that the chicken is cooked through, pierce the thickest
part of the thigh with a skewer – the juices should run clear.

4 Carve the chicken and serve
garnished with the roasted
lemon and lime and
extra herbs.

TIP

If you want to make a light gravy,
pour a little wine or stock into the
roasting tin and cook briefly over a
gentle heat until bubbling.

Nutritional information per serving:
Energy: 473 kcals/1960 kJ **Protein:** 35 g
Carbohydrate: 0 g **Fat:** 37 g **Fibre:** 0 g
Calcium: 47 mg **Iron:** 1 mg

Thai coconut chicken

Serves 4
Preparation: 20 minutes
Cooking: 45 minutes

1 green chilli, deseeded and
   roughly chopped

1 small onion, roughly chopped

3 garlic cloves, chopped

50 g/2 oz fresh coriander

2 teaspoons Thai fish sauce

¼ teaspoon ground turmeric

1 stalk lemon grass, roughly
   chopped

grated rind and juice of 1 lime

2 teaspoons caster sugar

15 g/½ oz fresh root ginger,
   roughly chopped

4 skinned, boneless chicken
   breasts

1 tablespoon refined groundnut
   oil

500 ml/17 fl oz chicken stock

400 ml/14 oz can coconut milk

salt and pepper

roughly chopped coriander, to
   garnish

1 To make the curry paste, put the chilli, onion, garlic, coriander, fish sauce, turmeric, lemon grass, lime rind and juice, sugar and ginger in a food processor or blender and process until smooth, scraping the mixture down from the sides of the bowl when necessary.

2 Cut the chicken into small pieces and season lightly. Heat the oil in a large saucepan and gently fry the chicken for 5 minutes.

3 Put the stock and curry mixture in a separate pan and bring to the boil. Cook uncovered for 15–20 minutes until most of the liquid has evaporated.

4 Add the chicken and coconut milk and cook for about 20 minutes until the chicken is very tender. Garnish with coriander and serve with fragrant rice or noodles.

Nutritional information per serving:
Energy: 214 kcals/900 kJ **Protein:** 29 g
Carbohydrate: 10 g **Fat:** 7 g **Fibre:** 0 g
Calcium: 60 mg **Iron:** 1 mg

Mushroom risotto

Serves 4
Preparation: 10 minutes
Cooking: about 30 minutes

50 g/2 oz butter

1 tablespoon olive oil

2 medium onions, finely
chopped

250 g/8 oz chestnut
mushrooms, thinly sliced

1 celery stick, chopped

375 g/12 oz risotto rice

2 garlic cloves, crushed

150 ml/¼ pint white wine

1 litre/1¾ pints chicken or
vegetable stock

100 g/3½ oz freshly grated
Parmesan cheese

salt and pepper

1 Melt half the butter with the oil in a large, heavy-based saucepan. Add the onions and fry gently for 2–3 minutes until softened. Add the mushrooms and fry quickly for 2 minutes. Drain the mushrooms and set aside.

2 Add the celery, rice and garlic, and cook, stirring, for 1 minute. Add the wine and continue to cook until it has evaporated.

3 Add 800 ml/1⅓ pints of the stock and cook uncovered, stirring frequently, for 20–25 minutes until the rice is tender and creamy, but still retains a little bite. Add more stock if necessary – the risotto should remain very juicy.

4 Stir in the mushrooms, half the cheese, the remaining butter and seasoning to taste. Serve immediately with the remaining cheese sprinkled on top.

VARIATION:

If you prefer not to include the wine, simply substitute additional stock.

Nutritional information per serving:
Energy: 630 kcals/2647 kJ **Protein:** 18 g
Carbohydrate: 88 g **Fat:** 23 g **Fibre:** 5 g
Calcium: 335 mg **Iron:** 2 mg

Roasted vegetable & red bean stew

Serves 5–6
Preparation: 20 minutes, plus overnight soaking
Cooking: about 1¼ hours

250 g/8 oz red kidney beans

1 kg/2 lb butternut squash

3 large red onions, cut into
   thin wedges

3 courgettes, thickly sliced

1 medium aubergine, about
   375 g/12 oz, cut into chunks

3 tablespoons olive oil

1 litre/1¾ pints vegetable stock

3 garlic cloves, slices

2 tablespoons chopped fresh
   oregano

3 bay leaves

2 tablespoons ground paprika

250 g/8 oz chestnut
   mushrooms, quartered

salt and pepper

soured cream, to serve
   (optional)

1 Soak the beans overnight in plenty of cold water. Drain, cover with fresh water and bring to the boil. Boil rapidly for 10 minutes, then drain.

2 Meanwhile, halve the squash, discard the seeds and cut away the skin. Cut the flesh into chunks and put in a large roasting tin with the onions, courgettes and aubergine. Drizzle with the oil, add a little seasoning and roast in a preheated oven, 220°C (425°F), Gas Mark 7, for about 1 hour, turning the vegetables occasionally until deep golden.

3 Meanwhile, put the beans in a large saucepan. Add the stock, garlic, herbs and paprika, and bring to the boil. Reduce the heat, cover and simmer gently for 30–40 minutes until the beans are tender.

4 Tip the roasted vegetables into the pan with the mushrooms and cook for a further 5 minutes until heated through. Serve in bowls, topped with spoonfuls of soured cream, if liked.

Nutritional information per serving:
Energy: 350 kcals/1490 kJ **Protein:** 18 g
Carbohydrate: 55 g **Fat:** 9 g **Fibre:** 17 g
Calcium: 215 mg **Iron:** 7 mg

Strawberry meringue roulade

Serves 6–8
Preparation: 20 minutes, plus cooling
Cooking: 30 minutes

4 medium egg whites

125 g/4 oz caster sugar

1 teaspoon white wine vinegar

1 teaspoon vanilla extract

25 g/1 oz flaked almonds

400 g/13 oz ripe strawberries

150 ml/¼ pint double cream

4 tablespoons Grand Marnier
  or other orange-flavoured
  liqueur

icing sugar for dusting

VARIATION:

This luxurious dessert can be adapted for any fruit, depending on what is in season – plump summer berries, juicy soft peaches and plums or a range of tropical fruits all make a delicious filling.

1 Line a 33 x 23 cm/13 x 9 inch Swiss roll tin with baking parchment. Whisk the egg whites in a thoroughly clean bowl until stiff. Gradually whisk in the sugar, a tablespoonful at a time, whisking well after each addition until the mixture is stiff and glossy. Whisk in the vinegar and vanilla extract.

2 Turn the mixture into the prepared tin and spread to an even layer. Sprinkle with the flaked almonds. Bake in a preheated oven at 170°C (325°F), Gas Mark 3, for about 30 minutes until the surface is turning pale golden. Leave to cool in the tin.

3 Sprinkle a sheet of baking parchment with a little extra sugar and invert the meringue on to the paper. Peel away the lining paper from the meringue.

4 Thinly slice the strawberries. Whip the cream with the liqueur until it just holds its shape. Spread to within 1 cm/½ inch of the edges of the meringue. Scatter with the strawberries and roll up, starting from a short edge.

5 Slide on to a serving plate and chill until ready to serve, lightly dusted with icing sugar.

Nutritional information per serving:
Energy: 277 kcals/1156 kJ **Protein:** 4 g
Carbohydrate: 30 g **Fat:** 14 g **Fibre:** 2 g
Calcium: 35 mg **Iron:** <1 mg

Apricot & marzipan tart

225 g/7½ oz white rice flour

2 teaspoons ground cinnamon

100 g/3½ oz firm unsalted
   butter

1 egg yolk

100 g/3½ oz grated cooking
   apple (about 1 medium
   apple)

50 g/2 oz plus 2 tablespoons
   caster sugar

50 g/2 oz icing sugar

150 g/5 oz ground almonds

finely grated rind of 1 orange

1 egg, beaten

625 g/1¼ lb ripe apricots

25 g/1 oz flaked almonds

4 tablespoons apricot jam

1 Put the flour and cinnamon in a bowl with the butter, cut into small pieces, and rub in with the fingertips. Stir in the egg yolk, grated apple and 2 tablespoons of caster sugar, and mix to a dough.

2 Break off pieces of dough, flatten them between your hands and press into a 23 cm/9 inch round loose-base tin so that the tin is lined in sections. Trim off any excess around the top.

3 Mix together the remaining caster sugar, icing sugar, ground almonds and orange rind. Add the egg and mix to a paste. Pack the paste into the pastry case. Halve and stone the apricots and scatter over the filling. Scatter with the flaked almonds.

4 Bake in a preheated oven at 400°C (200°F), Gas Mark 6, for about 40 minutes until the pastry is golden and apricots are tender.

5 While the tart is cooking, melt the jam in a small pan with 1 tablespoon of water and use to glaze the apricots. Serve warm or cold with pouring cream.

Nutritional information per serving:
Energy: 610 kcals/2547 kJ **Protein:** 11 g
Carbohydrate: 70 g **Fat:** 32 g **Fibre:** 6 g
Calcium: 122 mg **Iron:** 3 mg

Caramel fruit pudding

Serves 6
Preparation: 20 minutes
Cooking: 1½ hours

50 g/2 oz unsalted butter

50 g/2 oz light muscovado
sugar

2 bananas, sliced

2 pears, cored and chopped

175 g/6 oz no-soak dried
apricots, chopped

finely grated rind and juice of 1
lemon

SPONGE:

100 g/3½ oz light muscovado
sugar

100 g/3½ oz unsalted butter,
softened

2 eggs

50 g/2 oz gluten-free flour

1 teaspoon Gluten-free baking
powder (see page 42)

1 teaspoon ground mixed spice

150 g/5 oz gluten-free
breadcrumbs

1 Grease and base line a 1.5 litre/2½ pint pudding basin. Dice the butter and mix with the sugar, half the prepared fruit and the lemon rind and juice. Tip into the basin.

2 For the sponge, put the sugar, butter, eggs, flour, baking powder and spice in a bowl and beat until smooth (don't worry if the mixture curdles at this stage). Stir in the breadcrumbs and the remaining fruit.

3 Spoon the mixture over the fruit in the basin and level the surface. Cover with a double thickness of greaseproof paper, pleated in the centre to allow for expansion, and tie under the rim with string. Trim off the excess paper, then cover with foil, scrunching the edges under the rim to seal the pudding.

4 Place in a roasting tin and half-fill with boiling water. Overwrap with a large sheet of foil and transfer to a preheated oven, 170°C (325°F), Gas Mark 3. Bake for 1½ hours.

5 Carefully take the basin from the tin and remove the greaseproof paper. Tip the pudding on to a serving plate and cut in wedges. Serve with cream, ice cream or yogurt.

Nutritional information per serving:
Energy: 514 kcals/2155 kJ **Protein:** 5 g
Carbohydrate: 67 g **Fat:** 27 g **Fibre:** 7 g
Calcium: 76 mg **Iron:** 2 mg

Sweet pancakes with citrus sauce

Serves 4–6
Preparation: 25 minutes
Cooking: about 20 minutes

2 oranges

40 g/1½ oz butter

50 g/2 oz rice flour

25 g/1 oz plus 1 tablespoon
   caster sugar

100 ml/3½ fl oz milk

2 eggs, separated

oil for frying

2 tablespoons lemon juice

2 tablespoons orange liqueur
   (optional)

6 scoops vanilla ice cream

1 Finely grate the rind from 1 orange. Melt 15 g/½ oz of the butter. Put the flour, orange rind, melted butter, 1 tablespoon of the sugar, the milk and the egg yolks in a mixing bowl and whisk until smooth.

2 In a separate bowl, whisk the egg whites until frothy and just beginning to hold their shape. Add to the bowl and stir in until combined (the mixture should be foamy but still quite loose).

3 Heat a little oil in a medium-sized crêpe pan, drain off the excess oil and pour a little of the batter into the pan so that it spreads into a round about 15 cm/6 inches in diameter. (If the batter is so thick that it doesn't run, spread it with the back of a dessertspoon.) Once golden on the underside, turn the pancake with a fish slice and cook until set enough to slide out of the pan. Keep pancakes warm while making the remainder, brushing the pan with a little more oil each time.

4 Squeeze the juice from the 2 oranges. Melt the remaining butter and sugar in a frying pan until the sugar has dissolved. Add the orange and lemon juice and let the mixture bubble for about 2 minutes until syrupy. Stir in the liqueur if using.

5 Fold the pancakes into quarters and place on serving plates. Pour the sauce over and serve immediately with ice cream.

Nutritional information per serving:
Energy: 460 kcals/1933 kJ   **Protein:** 9 g
Carbohydrate: 50 g   **Fat:** 26 g   **Fibre:** 1 g
Calcium: 204 mg   **Iron:** 1 mg

Cherry & almond clafoutis

Serves 4
Preparation: 10 minutes
Cooking: 25 minutes

425 g/14 oz can pitted black
    cherries

2 eggs

1 egg yolk

50 g/2 oz caster sugar

25 g/1 oz butter, melted

25 g/1 oz ground almonds

1 teaspoon vanilla extract

175 ml/6 fl oz milk

100 ml/3½ fl oz double cream

icing sugar for dusting

1 Lightly butter a 1 litre/1¾ pint shallow ovenproof dish. Drain the cherries thoroughly and scatter in the dish.

2 Whisk the eggs with the yolk and sugar until slightly thickened and frothy. Stir in the butter, ground almonds, vanilla, milk and cream to make a smooth batter.

3 Pour the mixture over the cherries, then bake in a preheated oven, 190°C (375°F), Gas Mark 5, for 25–30 minutes until golden and only just setting in the middle. Dust with icing sugar and serve warm.

VARIATION:

During their short season, fresh cherries can be used instead of tinned or jarred. Allow about 300 g/10 oz and remember to remove the stones first.

Nutritional information per serving:
Energy: 398 kcals/1697kJ   **Protein:** 8 g
Carbohydrate: 34 g   **Fat:** 27 g   **Fibre:** 2 g
Calcium: 115 mg   **Iron:** 4 mg

Christmas pudding

Serves 12
Preparation: 20 minutes
Cooking: 4 hours, plus 2 hours
reheating

250 g/8 oz dried figs or dates,
  chopped

250 g/8 oz no-soak prunes,
  chopped

1 kg/2 lb mixed dried fruit

50 g/2 oz stem ginger, finely
  chopped

125 g/4 oz dark muscovado
  sugar

finely grated rind and juice of 1
  orange

150 g/5 oz gluten-free
  breadcrumbs

75 g/3 oz unsalted butter,
  chilled

3 eggs

100 ml/3½ fl oz medium sherry

caster sugar for sprinkling

1 Mix together the fruits, ginger, sugar, orange rind and juice and breadcrumbs in a large bowl.

2 Grate the butter directly over the bowl, stirring in frequently as you work so that it does not cake together. Add the eggs and ale, mixing until evenly combined.

3 Lightly grease and line the base of a 1.8 litre/3 pint pudding basin, then pack the mixture in, levelling the surface with the back of a spoon.

4 Cover with a double thickness of greaseproof paper, pleated in the centre to allow for expansion, and tie under the rim with string. Trim off the excess paper, then cover with foil, scrunching the edges under the rim to seal the pudding.

5 Put the pudding in a large, heavy-based saucepan and add boiling water to come halfway up the sides of the basin. Cover with a lid and steam gently for 4 hours, topping up with more boiling water if necessary. Leave to cool.

6 To reheat, steam as above for 2 hours. Loosen the edges of the pudding with a knife, then turn on to a serving plate. Serve sprinkled with caster sugar.

Nutritional information per serving:
Energy: 468 kcals/1980 kJ **Protein:** 5 g
Carbohydrate: 96 g **Fat:** 9 g **Fibre:** 11 g
Calcium: 137 mg **Iron:** 4 mg

Coffee & almond trifle

Serves 6
Preparation: 15 minutes

100 ml/3½ fl oz **strong black coffee, cooled**

6 tablespoons **Kahlua or other coffee-flavoured liqueur**

200 g/7 oz **full-fat cream cheese**

500 ml/17 fl oz **good-quality, creamy custard**

200 g/7 oz **homemade (see page 118) or ready-made almond macaroons**

50 g/2 oz **plain or milk chocolate, coarsely grated**

25 g/1 oz **flaked almonds, lightly toasted**

1 Mix the coffee with the liqueur in a jug.

2 Beat the cream cheese in a bowl to soften, then gradually beat in the custard until the mixture is completely smooth.

3 Arrange half the macaroons in the base of a 1.3 litre/2¼ pint glass serving dish and drizzle with half the coffee mixture. Put the remaining macaroons in a single layer on a plate and drizzle the remaining syrup over them.

4 Scatter with half the chocolate and half the almonds over the biscuits in the bowl. Spoon over half the cheese mixture.

5 Reserve a tablespoonful each of the chocolate and almonds for decoration. Layer the syrup steeped macaroons, chocolate and almonds in the dish. Pile the remaining cheese mixture on top and scatter with the reserved chocolate and almonds. Chill until ready to serve.

Nutritional information per serving:
Energy: 500 kcals/2093 kJ **Protein:** 8 g
Carbohydrate: 45 g **Fat:** 31 g **Fibre:** 2 g
Calcium: 186 mg **Iron:** 1 mg

Summer pudding

Serves 6–8
Preparation: 20 minutes, plus chilling
Cooking: 5 minutes

10 slices white gluten-free bread

800 g/1½ lb mixed summer fruits, such as redcurrants, blackcurrants, blackberries, strawberries or raspberries

100 g/3½ oz caster sugar

pouring cream or Greek yogurt, to serve

1 Put three bread slices to one side. Use the rest to line the base and sides of 1.2 litre/2 pint pudding basin, overlapping them to make a case.

2 Remove the stalks from the redcurrants and blackcurrants, if using, and hull the strawberries, halving any large ones. Tip into a large heavy-based saucepan and add the sugar. Heat gently for about 5 minutes, stirring frequently until the juices flow and the sugar has dissolved.

3 Using a large spoon, fill the bread-lined basin with the fruit, reserving any juice left in the pan. Place the remaining bread over the surface, trimming to fit. The bread should be soaked in juices, so pour over a little more juice if the bread seems dry. Cover and chill for at least 8 hours or overnight. Pour any remaining juice into a small jug.

4 To serve, loosen around the edges with a knife and invert on to a flat plate. Serve in wedges with cream or yogurt and extra juice if liked.

Nutritional information per serving:
Energy: 295 kcals/1240 kJ **Protein:** 3 g
Carbohydrate: 51 g **Fat:** 10 g **Fibre:** 8 g
Calcium: 76 mg **Iron:** 1 mg

Pannacotta with blueberry sauce

Serves 6
Preparation: 25 minutes

1½ teaspoons powdered
   gelatine or vegetarian
   gelling agent
300 ml/½ pint mascarpone
   cheese
300 ml/½ pint double cream
finely grated rind of 1 orange
   plus 2 teaspoons juice
125 g/4 oz caster sugar
2 teaspoons vanilla extract

SAUCE:
250 g/8 oz blueberries
1 tablespoon icing sugar

1 Sprinkle the gelatine over 3 tablespoons of water in a small bowl and set aside. Lightly oil six small dariole or individual metal pudding moulds.

2 Put the mascarpone in a saucepan with the cream, orange rind, sugar and vanilla, and bring just to the boil. Remove from the heat and add the gelatine. Stir thoroughly until the gelatine has completely dissolved.

3 Pour the cream mixture into the moulds and chill for several hours, or overnight until set.

4 Put the blueberries in a bowl and pierce all over with a fork to let the juices run a little. Add the icing sugar and orange juice, and mix together. Chill until ready to serve.

5 To serve, loosen the edges of the moulds with a knife and then shake them out on to individual plates. Spoon the blueberry sauce all around.

Nutritional information per serving:
Energy: 530 kcals/2208 kJ **Protein:** 5 g
Carbohydrate: 30 g **Fat:** 44 g **Fibre:** 3 g
Calcium: 53 mg **Iron:** 1 mg

Lemony polenta cake

Serves 6
Preparation: 10 minutes
Cooking: 30 minutes

175 g/6 oz **unsalted butter,**
   softened

250 g/8 oz **golden caster sugar**

125 g/4 oz **ground almonds**

2 eggs, **beaten**

finely grated rind and juice of 3
   lemons

75 g/3 oz **polenta flour**

50 g/2 oz **gluten-free plain**
   flour

½ teaspoon **Gluten-free baking**
   powder (see page 42)

2 tablespoons **flaked almonds**

1 Grease and line a 15 cm/6 inch spring-form tin with greaseproof paper. Beat together the butter and 175 g/6 oz of the sugar until pale and creamy. Stir in the almonds, eggs and rind and juice of 1 lemon.

2 Add the flours and baking powder, and stir in gently until combined. Turn into the tin, level the surface and sprinkle with the flaked almonds. Bake in a preheated oven, 180ºC (350ºF), Gas Mark 4, for about 30 minutes until risen and just firm.

3 Meanwhile, put the remaining lemon rind and juice in a small pan with the remaining sugar and heat gently until the sugar dissolves. Spoon over the cake and serve warm.

TIP

This crumbly almond sponge, dripping with a tangy, lemon syrup, is great with a cup of coffee. Alternatively, top with cream or yogurt for a tempting dessert.

Nutritional information per serving:
Energy: 598 kcals/2490 kJ **Protein:** 9 g
Carbohydrate: 55 g **Fat:** 39 g **Fibre:** 3 g
Calcium: 104 mg **Iron:** 2 mg

Almond macaroons

Makes about 20
Preparation: 10 minutes
Cooking: 15–20 minutes

2 egg whites

100 g/3½ oz golden caster
sugar

125 g/4 oz ground almonds

blanched almonds, to decorate

1 Line a large baking sheet with baking parchment. Whisk the egg whites until stiff. Gradually whisk in the sugar, a spoonful at a time, until the mixture is thick and glossy. Stir in the ground almonds.

2 Spoon the mixture into a large polythene bag, squeezing it gently into a corner. Snip off the corner of the bag so the mixture can be piped on to the baking sheet.

3 Pipe small rounds about 4 cm/1½ inches in diameter, spacing them slightly apart. Press a blanched almond into the top of each one.

4 Bake in a preheated oven, 180°C (350°F), Gas Mark 4, for 15–20 minutes until only just firm. Leave on the paper to cool.

TIP

If you would prefer not to pipe the mixture, simply drop spoonfuls on to the baking sheet. These classic, chewy teatime favourites can be served as they are or scribbled with melted chocolate.

Nutritional information per macaroon:
Energy: 62 kcals/260 kJ **Protein:** 2 g
Carbohydrate: 6 g **Fat:** 4 g **Fibre:** 1 g
Calcium: 16 mg **Iron:** 0 mg

Lemon-glazed shortbread

Serves 10–12
Preparation: 10 minutes
Cooking: 35 minutes

125 g/4 oz ground rice

100 g/3½ oz gluten-free flour

finely grated rind of 1 lemon
   plus 2½ teaspoons juice

100 g/3½ oz lightly salted
   butter

50 g/2 oz caster sugar

75 g/3 oz icing sugar

VARIATION:

You can use orange instead of the lemon, or leave out the fruit and simply dust generously with icing sugar instead.

1 Grease a 20 cm/8 inch round, loose-based sandwich tin. Put the ground rice, flour and lemon rind in a food processor. Add the butter, cut into small pieces, and process until the mixture resembles breadcrumbs.

2 Add the caster sugar and blend again until the mixture starts to bind together. (Alternatively, put the rice, flour and lemon rind in a bowl, add the butter and rub in with the fingertips before adding the sugar.) Turn into the tin and press down with the fingertips until the surface is level.

3 Bake in a preheated oven, 170°C (325°F), Gas Mark 3, for about 35 minutes until pale golden. Leave in the tin for 5 minutes, then lift the base out of the tin and slide the biscuit on to a wire rack. Mark into small wedges.

4 Beat together the lemon juice and icing sugar to make a thin icing with the consistency of pouring cream. Drizzle over the shortbread and leave to set. Store in an airtight container for up to 4 days.

Nutritional information per serving:
Energy: 200 kcals/855 kJ **Protein:** 1 g
Carbohydrate: 32 g **Fat:** 8 g **Fibre:** 0 g
Calcium: 5 mg **Iron:** 0 mg

Chunky rich fruit cake

Serves 24
Preparation: 20 minutes
Cooking: about 1¼ hours

300 ml/½ pint apple juice

15 g/½ oz dried yeast

1 cooking apple, cored and
   roughly chopped

125 g/4 oz gluten-free flour

250 g/8 oz rice flour

2 teaspoons Gluten-free baking
   powder (see page 42)

1 tablespoon ground mixed
   spice

25 g/1 oz butter, melted

1 medium carrot, finely grated

300 g/10 oz luxury mixed dried
   fruit

100 g/3½ oz no-soak prunes,
   chopped

100 g/3½ oz no-soak dried
   apricots, chopped

125 g/4 oz blanched almonds,
   roughly chopped

1 Grease and line a 20 cm/8 inch round or 18 cm/7 inch square cake tin. Gently warm the apple juice in a small pan until tepid. Remove from the heat and sprinkle over the yeast. Leave for 5 minutes until the mixture is frothy. Transfer to a food processor or blender, add the apple and process until the apple is almost smooth.

2 Put the flours, baking powder and spice into a mixing bowl. Add the butter, carrot and yeast mixture, and stir until combined.

3 Add all the dried fruit and the almonds, and stir well. Turn into the prepared tin and bake in a preheated oven, 170°C (325°F), Gas Mark 3, for about 1¼ hours or until the surface is firm to the touch and a skewer inserted into the centre comes out clean. Leave to cool in the tin.

4 Wrap in foil and store in a cool place until needed.

TIP

For a special occasion, you can add alcohol to the recipe. After baking, pierce the surface of the cake with a skewer and drizzle with 4–5 tablespoons of brandy, rum or orange liqueur. Wrap and store.

Nutritional information per serving:
Energy: 153 kcals/640 kJ   **Protein:** 3 g
Carbohydrate: 27 g   **Fat:** 4 g   **Fibre:** 3 g
Calcium: 40 mg   **Iron:** 1 mg

Very chocolaty brownies

Makes 18
Preparation: 10 minutes
Cooking: 30 minutes

200 g/7 oz milk chocolate

200 g/7 oz plain chocolate

200 g/7 oz unsalted butter

3 eggs

175 g/6 oz light muscovado
 sugar

75 g/3 oz gluten-free flour

2 teaspoons Gluten-free baking
 powder (see page 42)

200 g/7 oz walnut pieces

VARIATION:

Chop the walnuts finely if you
prefer, or substitute almonds or
macadamia nuts for a milder
flavour.

1 Grease and line a 28 x 20 cm/11 x 8 inch shallow baking tin
with baking parchment. Chop the milk chocolate into small
chunks. Melt the plain chocolate with the butter in a small
bowl set over hot water.

2 Beat together the eggs and sugar until turning foamy. Stir in
the melted chocolate mixture.

3 Sift the flour and baking powder into the bowl. Add the
chopped chocolate and walnut pieces and fold the ingredients
together gently. Pour the mixture into the baking tin.

4 Bake in a preheated oven at 190°C (375°F), Gas Mark 5, for
30 minutes until a sugary crust has formed on the surface but
the mixture gives slightly underneath (it will firm up slightly as
it cools, so avoid the temptation to cook for longer). Leave to
cool in the tin.

5 Cut into squares and store in an airtight container in a cool
place for up to 6 days.

Nutritional information per serving:
Energy: 343 kcals/1428 kJ **Protein:** 5 g
Carbohydrate: 28 g **Fat:** 24 g **Fibre:** 1 g
Calcium: 56 mg **Iron:** 1 mg

Fruited teacake

300 g/10 oz mixed dried fruit

75 g/3 oz dark muscovado
   sugar

finely grated rind of 1 orange

150 ml/¼ pint orange juice

100 g/3½ oz gluten-free flour

½ teaspoon Gluten-free baking
   powder (see page 42)

1 egg, lightly beaten

1 Grease a 500 g/1 lb loaf tin. Put the dried fruit, sugar, orange
rind and juice in a small, heavy-based saucepan. Bring to the
boil and let the mixture bubble for about 5 minutes until the
liquid is thickened and syrupy. Tip into a mixing bowl and
leave for 10 minutes.

2 Add the flour, baking powder and egg, and stir until
combined. Turn into the tin and bake in a preheated oven,
180°C (350°F), Gas Mark 4, for about 40 minutes until slightly
risen and firm to the touch. Transfer to a wire rack to cool.

VARIATION:

For flavour variations, try
lemon or grapefruit instead of
the orange and add a little
spice such as ground cinnamon,
cloves or ginger.

Nutritional information per serving:
Energy: 200 kcals/853 kJ **Protein:** 3 g
Carbohydrate: 48 g **Fat:** 1 g **Fibre:** 3 g
Calcium: 42 mg **Iron:** 1 mg

Rich chocolate & hazelnut gateau

Serves 10–12
Preparation: 20 minutes, plus cooling
Cooking: 30 minutes

200 g/7 oz plain chocolate

75 ml/3 fl oz milk

175 g/6 oz very soft unsalted
  butter

175 g/6 oz golden caster sugar

175 g/6 oz ground hazelnuts

50 g/2 oz gluten-free flour

5 eggs, separated

ICING:

100 g/3½ oz plain chocolate

15 g/½ oz butter

25 g/1 oz blanched hazelnuts,
  toasted and roughly chopped

1 Grease and line a 23 cm/9 inch round cake tin. Melt the chocolate with the milk, stirring occasionally until smooth.

2 Transfer to a mixing bowl and add the butter, sugar, ground nuts, flour and egg yolks. Stir until well combined.

3 In a separate bowl, whisk the egg whites until peaking. Using a large metal spoon, transfer a quarter of the whites to the chocolate mixture and fold in. Fold in the remainder.

4 Turn into the prepared tin and level the surface. Bake in a preheated oven, 180°C (350°F), Gas Mark 4, for 30 minutes or until the surface feels just firm to the touch. Leave to cool in the tin before turning out.

5 To decorate the cake, melt together the chocolate and butter and spread over the top. Sprinkle the chopped hazelnuts aroung the top edges of the cake. Leave to set.

Nutritional information per serving:
Energy: 560 kcals/2330 kJ   **Protein:** 8 g
Carbohydrate: 44 g   **Fat:** 40 g   **Fibre:** 2 g
Calcium: 67 mg   **Iron:** 2 mg

Index

Acknowledgements

Photographic Acknowledgements in Source Order

Corbis UK Ltd/David Raymer 37
Getty Images/James Darell 14 /Grant V. Faint 7 /Gerd George 28
/Bay Hippisley 4 /Howard Kingsnorth 20 /Tony Latham 12 /Frederic
Tousche 6
Octopus Publishing Group Limited/Stephen Conroy 15 detail 11
/David Jordan 15 detail 5, 23, 27, 29, 35 /Graham Kirk 15 detail 14,
/William Lingwood 10 /Neil Mersh 30 /Sean Myers 15 detail 9
/Peter Pugh-Cook 11, 15 detail 13, 22, 24, 25 /William Reavell 5 top left,
5 bottom right, 5 bottom left, 5 bottom centre, 8 bottom, 15 detail 1,
15 detail 2, 15 detail 3, 15 detail 4, 15 detail 6, 15 detail 8, 15 detail 10,
15 detail 12, 19, 20 bottom left, 21 top left, 21 bottom left, 26
/Craig Robertson front cover top left, front cover top right, front
cover top centre, front cover bottom left, front cover bottom right,
front cover bottom centre, back cover top, back cover bottom, 1 left,
1 right, 1 centre, 3 top, 3 centre bottom, 3 centre top, 3 bottom, 5 top
right, 8 top left, 8 centre left, 8 top right, 8 centre right, 16, 18, 20
centre left, 33, 34 top, 34 bottom, 39, 40 top right, 40 bottom left, 41,
43, 47, 50-51, 53, 57, 61, 65, 66, 71, 75, 79, 81, 85, 89, 91, 93, 97, 101, 105,
109, 115, 117, 121, 125 /Gareth Sambidge 32 /Simon Smith 15 detail 7, 21
centre /Ian Wallace 36 /Mark Winwood 31
Photodisc 13
Science Photo Library/Sheila Terry 17

Executive Editor **Nicola Hill**
Editor **Rachel Lawrence**
Executive Art Editor **Leigh Jones**
Designer **Tony Truscott**
Production Controller **Louise Hall**
Picture Researcher **Christine Junemann**

Special Photography **Craig Robertson**
Home Economist **Sarah O'Brien**